Jeffery V. Bailey, CFA
Dayton Hudson Corporation

David E. Tierney
Richards & Tierney, Inc.

Controlling Misfit Risk in Multiple-Manager Investment Programs

The Research Foundation of
The Institute of Chartered Financial Analysts

Research Foundation Publications

Controlling Misfit Risk in Multiple-Manager Investment Programs

The Institute of Chartered Financial Analysts is a subsidiary of the Association for Investment Management and Research.

ISBN 0-943205-43-3

Printed in the United States of America

March 1998

Editorial Staff
Bette Collins and Charlene Semer
Editors

Fiona D. Russell
Assistant Editor

Jaynee M. Dudley
Production Manager

Christine P. Martin
Production Coordinator

Lois A. Carrier and Diane B. Hamshar
Composition

Mission

The Research Foundation's mission is to identify, fund, and publish research that is relevant to the AIMR Global Body of Knowledge and useful for AIMR member investment practitioners and investors.

About the Authors

Jeffery V. Bailey, CFA, is Director of Benefit Finance at Dayton Hudson Corporation, where he oversees the investment of the company's defined-benefit and defined-contribution plan assets. Formerly, Mr. Bailey was a principal at Richards & Tierney, Inc., where he directed the firm's performance attribution services. Prior to joining Richards & Tierney, he was assistant director of the Minnesota State Board of Investment, where he headed the external manager operations and developed investment policy for the board's various funds. Mr. Bailey has published numerous articles on pension management, and he is co-author, with William Sharpe and Gordon Alexander, of the textbooks *Investments* and *Fundamentals of Investments*. Mr. Bailey holds a B.A. in economics from Oakland University and an M.A. in economics and an M.B.A in finance from the University of Minnesota.

David E. Tierney is cofounder and a principal of Richards & Tierney, Inc., a Chicago-based pension consulting firm that specializes in applying quantitative risk-control techniques to enhance the performance of plan sponsor portfolios. Previously, Mr. Tierney was administrative manager of the Investments area for the Amoco Corporation pension fund. At Amoco, he directed and coordinated the activities of the fund's investment managers, controlled the fund's accounting and auditing functions, analyzed the performance of the fund's managers, and conducted research into methods of pension management. In addition, he has taught at the University of Chicago Graduate School of Business. Mr. Tierney holds a B.S. in engineering science from Northwestern University and an M.S. and Ph.D. in applied statistics from the University of Wisconsin.

Contents

Foreword

In the not-too-distant past, portfolio managers were considered successful if they merely produced returns that were larger than those generated by their peers. As we reach the beginning of a new millennium, however, we now know that such simple return comparisons are inadequate barometers of performance. Indeed, one of the most fundamental contributions that financial theory has made to financial practice in the past three decades has been the explicit recognition that an investor's return is, in part, compensation for bearing risk. Thus, any metric that purports to judge the quality of a manager's investment acumen must do so on a risk-adjusted basis.

Although straightforward in concept, calculating risk-adjusted returns is hardly a trivial matter. What, for instance, is the appropriate measure of portfolio risk (beta, sigma, multiple-factor loadings)? What is the appropriate time frame for measuring performance? What is the appropriate benchmark or peer group against which the manager's performance should be evaluated? What adjustments are necessary if the portfolio in question has allocations to several different asset classes? Does the manager's investment style dictate the use of one measure rather than another? Should selection and allocation effects be accounted for separately? How does the use of multiple managers in one portfolio complicate the measurement process?

In this monograph, Jeffery Bailey and David Tierney bring their considerable experience and expertise to bear on many aspects of these questions. In particular, they consider the challenges faced by the sponsor of an institutional portfolio that uses several managers, each with a potentially different investment style, to cover a single asset class. They begin with the important observation that the decision to use multiple managers is really an element of the sponsor's investment policy decision; how the sponsor allocates funds across managers with different styles will, to a substantial degree, determine the portfolio's ultimate performance for a short- to intermediate-term horizon. Related to this observation, the dimension of the allocation decision is the sponsor's choice of the appropriate investment opportunity set—or target—for the relevant asset class.

In the simplest terms, the basic question that this research addresses can be posed as follows: What is the best way to manage the problem created by the performance differential between the portfolio's target and the benchmark used to proxy that target? The authors call this difference "the misfit problem," and their empirical work suggests that the cost it imposes on the investor can be significant. Chief among the solutions they propose to limit misfit is the use of a "dynamic completeness fund" (DCF), which they define as a zero-wealth hedge fund whose investment weights are determined by the under- or overallocations in the benchmark relative to the target. They demonstrate how misfit can be eliminated by combining the DCF with the sponsor's underlying portfolio.

This monograph is not labeled a tutorial, but it offers the reader a practical, instructive guide to many of the most important aspects of measuring investment performance. The early chapters include forays into such topics as policy determination, style analysis, target and benchmark selection, information ratios, the "algebra" of portfolio design, and the DCF construction process with single or multiple managers. Chapter 4, which contains case studies that summarize the actual experiences three plan sponsors have had in implementing a DCF program, is especially rewarding. The final chapters extend the basic concepts in the sort of useful, if sometimes challenging, ways that are necessary to provide the reader with a complete treatment of the topic.

Bailey and Tierney have done an excellent job of defining the questions and providing answers to a problem that will only grow in prominence in future years. This work represents a compelling marriage between theoretical grounding and practical insights that should help make it a widely used tool in the investment community. The Research Foundation is quite pleased to bring it to your attention.

Keith C. Brown, CFA
Research Director
Research Foundation of the
Institute of Chartered Financial Analysts

Dedication

From the late 1970s through the early 1980s, I was privileged to have worked for Philipp W. Binzel at Amoco Corporation. Phil was an early corporate proponent of both the application of modern portfolio theory and the empowerment of employees. He held to the belief that there was always more to learn, more to experience, more improvements to be made, and more challenges to be met. With his urging and enthusiasm, I first presented the concepts behind what we today call the dynamic completeness fund at a conference in Scottsdale, Arizona, in the fall of 1979. Betty, Phil's wife, also had a hand in the history of DCFs, for she is the one responsible for coining the term "completeness."

Phil retired from Amoco in 1986 and, unfortunately, passed away March 20, 1995, at the age of 71. With great thanks to Phil and his family for all their encouragement and support through the years, I dedicate this monograph in his memory.

David E. Tierney

Preface

An investment issue that plagues many plan sponsors is the risk associated with unintended style biases. Plan sponsors typically have some target index against which the results of their investments in a particular asset category are compared. Style bias (or misfit) can cause a plan sponsor's portfolio managers, in aggregate, to underperform the target despite each individual manager performing well against his or her assigned benchmark. Often, the result is unproductive hirings and firings of managers. This monograph presents an analytical framework for evaluating and treating misfit risk.

We first describe recent developments in the efforts to manage the risk associated with the allocation to investment styles within an asset category. In particular, we examine a risk-control technique known as a *dynamic completeness fund*. (For quick reference, the reader can turn to the Glossary for the specific definitions we use for this and other terms first given in italics.) We begin with a discussion of several essential completeness fund concepts and provide empirical evidence regarding the relative magnitudes of style and active-management risks in plan sponsors' domestic equity portfolios. We then discuss possible approaches to controlling style risk. Each approach has certain advantages and disadvantages, which plan sponsors should evaluate before making a decision. We next describe the construction process for a dynamic completeness fund (DCF) and present case studies that describe the implementation of DCFs by several plan sponsors. From that point, we move to the theoretical foundations of completeness funds and present insights into more-complex DCF relationships. Finally, we consider several examples of extended completeness fund applications and offer some predictions about the course of efforts to control style bias in multiple-manager investment programs.

Our understanding of style bias has benefited greatly from ideas arising during discussions with many of our fellow practitioners—academics, consultants, investment managers, and plan sponsors. In particular, the clients of Richards & Tierney, Inc., have been an invaluable source of criticisms (usually constructive) and suggestions. We would particularly like to thank Howard Bicker, Ron Boller, Doug Gorence, and Ray Schmalz for their contributions. Their pension funds have had the benefit (and borne the pain) of being guinea pigs in the effort to improve ways of systematically measuring and controlling style bias. We would also like to thank Ed Kunzman and Sandi Weiskrich for their research assistance, Ann Posey for her seemingly endless energy and creative ideas, and Keith Brown for his comments and suggestions. Finally, this monograph would not have been possible without the support of the Research Foundation of the Institute of Chartered Financial Analysts.

Jeffery V. Bailey, CFA
David E. Tierney, Ph.D.

1. Basic Completeness Fund Concepts

One fundamental lesson of modern capital market theory is that investors operate in a world of returns *and* risks. Investors, of course, tend to focus their attention on the former because returns are tangible and the most visible indicator of an investment program's success. Risks, however, are difficult to define, let alone measure. Yet, investors ignore risk at their own peril.

"Owners" of large pools of assets (broadly, the *plan sponsors*) have long been cognizant of the biggest single source of risk in their investment programs, namely, the systematic exposure resulting from their allocations to broad asset categories, such as stocks and bonds. Plan sponsors control systematic risk by establishing long-term asset allocation policies for their investment programs. Indeed, only the rare plan sponsor has failed to adopt some type of formal asset allocation policy.

Separating the Sources of Total Fund Risk

Plan sponsors have increasingly come to understand that investment risk is a multifaceted concept. Although systematic (or market) risk is by far the greatest source of portfolio return variability, it is not the only one. Two other sources are risk associated with manager investment styles and risk derived from managers' active investment strategies.

If we examined a typical sponsor's domestic equity portfolio, we would separate the sources of return variability as shown in Figure 1.1. By far the largest portion of the domestic equity portfolio's return variability comes from simply being invested in the asset category. Yet, even if domestic equity's portion of the total fund is given, the plan sponsor must still face the issue of return variability related to style and active management. A multibillion-dollar pension fund with a standard allocation to domestic equity exposes tens of millions of dollars to returns influenced by these two sources of risk.

Figure 1.1. Domestic Equity Sources of Return Variability

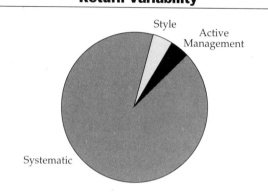

Exhibit 1.1 presents a generalized historical view of how plan sponsors have approached risk control in their investment programs during the past three decades. In the 1970s, the investment of sponsors' assets was left in the hands of balanced fund managers. These managers controlled the plans' entire risk profiles through asset allocation (systematic risk), through the selection of broad investment approaches within asset categories (*style risk*), and through the application of specific investment strategies within selected investment styles (*active-management risk*). Although the balanced managers did not literally segregate their investment decisions in such a precise manner, the results were effectively the same.

By the early 1980s, virtually all plan sponsors had taken charge of the asset allocation decision, thereby assuming responsibility for the control of systematic risk. They replaced the balanced managers with an array of specialty managers within each asset category. Nevertheless, during this time, sponsors rarely made explicit attempts to control the mix of investment styles within their investment programs.

Exhibit 1.1. Division of Responsibility for Total Portfolio Risk Control

Source of Risk	1970s	1980s	1990s
Systematic	Manager	Plan sponsor	Plan sponsor
Style bias	Manager	Manager	Plan sponsor
Active management	Manager	Manager	Manager

In the 1990s, plan sponsors have undertaken more concerted efforts to identify the investment styles of their money managers and to control the style risk and active-management risk to which those managers expose the sponsors' investment programs.[1]

In this monograph, we describe recent developments in the effort to manage the risk associated with the allocation to investment styles within an asset category. In particular, we examine a risk-control technique known as a *dynamic completeness fund* (DCF). The concepts and techniques discussed here can be applied to any asset category in which plan sponsors retain multiple managers to invest in publicly traded securities and in which those managers pursue a diverse set of investment styles. Our focus, however, is on U.S. domestic equities—for several reasons. First, U.S. common stocks constitute the largest portion of most plan sponsors' investment programs. Second, as a broadly defined asset category, U.S. common stocks experience relatively high return variability compared with some other asset categories, such as domestic fixed income. Third, because of data availability and the research efforts of many organizations, U.S. common stocks have been the most thoroughly investigated of all asset categories. In particular, reliable statistical models have been developed that help measure and control domestic equity risk.

Investment Policy

The old adage "If you don't know where you're going, any road will do" aptly applies to the investment of plan assets. Without a clear sense of why the plan exists and how it is expected to achieve its objectives, a plan sponsor may gravitate toward the most recently successful investment strategies. Portfolio insurance offers an example of this tendency. As equity values rose rapidly during the mid-1980s, the idea of protecting against a market decline gained popularity. Many sponsors entered into synthetic put strategies, commonly referred to as portfolio insurance, as a means of avoiding losses in severe stock market downturns while at the same time participating in further market

---

[1] Recently, "global-mandate" managers have gained increased attention. Plan sponsors assign such managers the authority to allocate funds across asset categories and invest within those asset categories. Bringing the manager–plan sponsor relationship full circle, these arrangements (often called "strategic partnerships") resemble the old balanced manager assignments. The success and longevity of these new relationships remains unproven. Nevertheless, we optimistically (perhaps overly so) expect that sponsors will continue to apply their accumulated knowledge of style risk and active-management risk to control the overall risk profile of their investment programs, even when entering into these strategic partnerships. Moreover, we hope that the global-mandate managers likewise will seek to improve their investment products by applying these risk-management concepts.

appreciation. Some sponsors claimed that such strategies could be implemented at a zero (or even negative) cost.

Portfolio insurance failed spectacularly during the stock market crash of October 1987. Consequently, most plan sponsor users of portfolio insurance abandoned it shortly thereafter. (One may argue whether portfolio insurance managers effectively implemented the strategy.[2]) Nevertheless, the concept itself is not inherently flawed. The disappointing results derived from a misunderstanding on the part of sponsors regarding how portfolio insurance fit with their funds' investment objectives. Funds with long-term time horizons were effectively making short-run market-timing decisions using portfolio insurance.

The frequent hiring and firing of money managers provides another example of the lack of long-run vision on the part of many plan sponsors. Usually, such manager turnover is a sign of dissatisfaction with recent performance relative to broad market indexes. Yet, the performance of a given U.S. common stock manager relative to the S&P 500 Index over three to five years (the length of a standard evaluation period) is a function of many factors, few of which directly relate to the manager's investment skills. Our experience has been that the failure of sponsors to understand how investment styles influence managers' investment results and how those styles fit into the plans' investment programs are the most common causes of unnecessary and counterproductive manager turnover.

What is missing in these examples and the many others that could be cited is not a lack of good intentions on the part of plan sponsors. Rather, it is the absence of a well-formulated and consistently applied investment policy. What do we mean by the term *investment policy*? Investment policy is a combination of philosophy and planning. It expresses the sponsor's attitudes toward a number of important pension-management issues: What is the purpose of our pension fund? How do we define success? How do we evaluate the performance of our investment program? The answers to these questions will likely differ among sponsors, depending on the financial circumstances of the sponsoring organizations and the diverse temperaments of the sponsors' decision makers.

---

[2] On an extraneous note, we believe that portfolio insurance failed because it required a market maker to provide continuous liquidity. In the futures market, no one is required to make a market, and thus, on that Monday in October 1987, the brokers simply closed their books and left the trading pits until such time as more rational pricing prevailed. The portfolio insurers were unable to trade at any price and were forced to suffer the consequences of firemen arriving at a fire and finding that the water hydrants had been turned off. The home (portfolio) that the firemen (portfolio insurers) were supposed to protect burned, even though the homeowner (the plan sponsor) had paid the municipal taxes for fire protection services.

Investment policy is also a form of long-term strategic planning. It delineates the specific goals the plan sponsor expects the fund to accomplish, and it describes how the sponsor foresees the fund realizing those goals. In this sense, investment policy comprises the set of guidelines and procedures that direct the long-term management of a plan's assets.

Plan sponsors' interpretations of precisely what constitutes investment policy may vary. Essentially, any relatively permanent set of procedures that guides the management of a plan's assets falls under the rubric of investment policy. A comprehensive investment policy, however, should address a group of issues that includes (but is not restricted to)

- the fund's mission,
- risk tolerance,
- policy asset mix,
- degree of active management,
- investment manager structure, and
- performance evaluation.

The broad topic of investment policy has been addressed elsewhere, and we will not repeat that discussion here.[3] Instead, our focus is on a specific element of investment policy, namely, the issue of investment manager structure. A plan sponsor that uses multiple active managers must determine the allocation of assets among those managers. As part of this process of *manager structuring*, the sponsor should be aware of the style risk that various allocation schemes present. By establishing an investment policy explicitly designed to manage style risk, the sponsor increases its chances of attaining successful investment results.

Asset Categories

When preparing an investment policy, plan sponsors typically separate the universe of investable securities into broad *asset categories*, such as domestic and foreign equities, real estate, venture capital, and so forth. Ideally, a manager would have complete information about all securities and create his or her portfolio accordingly. The complexity of the capital markets, however, has forced investment professionals to adopt a myopic approach to portfolio management, manifested by specialized skills related to specific types of securities. Being a successful U.S. stock manager is difficult enough, let alone being a successful manager of U.S. stocks *and* bonds. Even within investment firms that offer both bond and stock portfolio management, analysts and portfolio managers are assigned to specific asset categories and rarely overlap in their portfolio decision-making responsibilities.

---

[3]See, for example, Ambachtsheer (1986) and Ellis (1985).

The designation of asset categories is admittedly arbitrary. The distinction between certain broad asset categories, such as stocks and bonds, seems clear. What about more narrowly defined asset categories, such as investment-grade and high-yield bonds or U.S. and international stocks? Should non-U.S. stocks be divided further into regions or countries for purposes of asset category definition?

Conceptually, asset categories should be defined such that, on average, the correlation of returns between securities within an asset category is greater than the correlation of returns between securities among asset categories. As a practical matter, however, the marketplace designates asset categories. To the extent that defining the financial universe in terms of a particular set of asset categories serves the purposes of managers and plan sponsors, they will do so. When those distinctions no longer serve a purpose, investors will gradually adopt other categorizations. For example, the integration of the world's financial markets is a highly touted trend. Ultimately, investors may see no more distinction between a food-processing company domiciled in Japan and one in the United States, just as investors do not distinguish between such companies located in California or Michigan. For the time being, however, investors usually find it beneficial to separate U.S. companies from non-U.S. companies when making portfolio-construction decisions. Virtually all plan sponsors identify U.S. domestic equity and non-U.S. equity asset categories in their policy asset mixes.[4]

Asset Category Targets

Within a specific asset category, plan sponsors have some concept, either explicitly or implicitly, of the scope of their potential investments. In most cases, that scope is formalized by the selection of an *asset category target* (henceforth, referred to simply as the "target"). The target represents the set of feasible investment opportunities that the sponsor believes best achieves the purposes for which the asset category is included in the plan's investment policy. We can think of a target as the single portfolio in which the plan's assets would be placed were the sponsor required to passively manage all of its investments in that asset category.

Properties of a Valid Target. An appropriate target should satisfy three conditions:

- *It should be consistent with the plan sponsor's tolerance for risk.* If the target is too defensively or aggressively positioned relative to the sponsor's

---

[4]One empirical method of defining asset classes is presented in Greer (1997).

willingness to bear risk, then eventually the sponsor will be dissatisfied with either the returns on its investments in the asset category, the volatility of those returns, or both.

- *It should be preferred to all other alternative targets.* The expected long-run risk-adjusted returns from the target must be superior to other investable, passively managed alternatives. If not, then the plan sponsor has settled for an acknowledged inferior focal point for its investments in the asset category.

- *It should provide an investable alternative to existing investments in the asset category.* The plan sponsor must be able to own a passively managed portfolio that adequately tracks the target's performance, after deducting all associated fees and expenses.

Plan sponsors typically choose broad market indexes as their targets; for example, the S&P 500, the Russell 3000 Index, or the Wilshire 5000 Index are the preferred domestic equity targets. Not all market indexes possess the breadth required of an acceptable target. For example, the Dow Jones Industrial Average, although widely quoted as an indicator of domestic equity performance, represents a relatively narrow segment of the U.S. stock market. It is composed of the stocks of 30 large, mature corporations and fails to account for the performance of certain sectors of the economy. As a result, it does not adequately represent the investment opportunities available to investors in U.S. common stocks.

Some market indexes fail to satisfy the investability condition. For example, the Value Line Index is uninvestable because of the unusual method used to calculate its returns. An actual portfolio's return is the weighted average of the constituent securities' returns; the weights are the proportions of the portfolio invested in the individual securities. The return on the Value Line Index is based on the geometric average of its securities' returns. An actual portfolio containing the same securities as the Value Line Index cannot generate an equivalent return (except by chance), regardless of the weighting scheme applied.

Familiar Domestic Equity Targets. Table 1.1 compares financial characteristics of three broad market indexes that often serve as domestic equity targets. Exhibit 1.2 outlines the advantages and disadvantages of those market indexes for a plan sponsor selecting a target from among them. The information in Table 1.1 and Exhibit 1.2 indicates that the selection of a domestic equity target is not a simple decision. In the final analysis, the plan sponsor decision makers must answer the question: If all of the plan's domestic equity assets were to be passively managed, what is the single index that we would select to implement our investment program?

Table 1.1.   Financial Characteristics for Several Domestic Equity Asset Category Targets, June 1996

Characteristic	Wilshire 5000	Russell 3000	S&P 500
Number of stocks	7,014	3,000	500
Total market capitalization (trillions)	$7.1	$6.8	$5.0
Dividend yield	1.9%	2.0%	2.2%
P/B	3.6	3.6	3.7
P/E	18.1	17.9	18.0
Five-year growth in earnings per share	10.5	10.4	9.6
10-year average rate of return	14.2%	14.4%	15.0%

Exhibit 1.2. Advantages and Disadvantages of Several Domestic Equity Asset Category Targets

Index	Advantages	Disadvantages
Wilshire 5000	All inclusive (if priced) No ADRs Recognized	Variable composition REITs, MLPs, dual-class stocks No large non-U.S. ordinaries Thinly traded issues
Russell 3000	Deterministic selection criteria No ADRs Annual rebalancing Recognized	No large non-U.S. ordinaries REITs, MLPs, dual-class stocks No preannouncement of changes Ex-date dividend reinvestment
S&P 500	Long history Widely recognized Futures contracts Minimal changes Includes large non-U.S. ordinaries Excludes REITs, MLPs, dual-class stocks	Changes occur unexpectedly Nondeterministic selection Excludes many institution-held stocks

Note: ADRs = American Depositary Receipts; REITs = real estate investment trusts; MLPs = master limited partnerships.

Plan sponsors choose their targets from among broad market indexes based more on conventional wisdom than on thoughtful reflection. Market indexes do not incorporate specific restrictions that may impinge on a sponsor's investment program. In addition, market indexes often exclude certain types of securities in which a sponsor's managers regularly invest, and they may include other securities in which the managers rarely, if ever, invest.[5]

[5] On occasion, examples of the former include large American Depositary Receipts. On occasion, examples of the latter include various small-capitalization, illiquid issues.

8

Moreover, there are reasons to suspect that alternative well-diversified portfolios offer superior long-term risk–reward characteristics relative to standard market indexes.[6]

Plan sponsors might be better off creating custom targets designed to satisfy their own unique financial circumstances, risk tolerances, and long-run views of capital market risks and rewards. For example, consider a large electric utility company and its pension fund. Observing many other plan sponsors, the company begins with the S&P 500 as the target for its domestic equity investments. This company, however, decides to exclude both its stock and the stocks of other electric utility companies from the market index. The logic behind the company's decision is that it wants to avoid the magnified risk that adverse regulatory decisions will damage both its basic business and the performance of its pension fund. Furthermore, suppose the company's pension fund decision makers subscribe to the idea that, over the long run, on a risk-adjusted basis, high book/price stocks will outperform low book/price stocks. They could implement such beliefs by "tilting" the S&P 500 so that high-book/price stocks receive more weight in the custom target than do low-book/price stocks relative to those stocks' respective weights in the S&P 500.

The Investment Policy Functions of Targets. A target serves both prospective and retrospective functions in a plan sponsor's investment policy. In its retrospective role, the target is an evaluation tool. It is the benchmark against which to assess the performance of the plan's *aggregate* investments in the asset class. The plan sponsor should deviate from a passive investment in the target only if it believes that alternative investment strategies offer positive incremental returns relative to the risk incurred in pursuing those strategies. In hindsight, then, the sponsor's investments in the asset category are successful only if they at least match the target's returns (after all fees and expenses) on a risk-adjusted basis.

In its prospective role, the target is a planning tool. It possesses a risk profile that the investment styles of the plan sponsor's managers within the asset category should display, in aggregate. Recall that the target reflects the sponsor's preferred risk posture, exclusive of active management. Therefore, whether one views risk in a capital asset pricing model (CAPM), arbitrage pricing theory, or some other framework, unless the aggregate of the managers' investment styles is similar in risk to the target, a fundamental inconsistency exists.

---

[6]For example, see BARRA (1989), Grinold (1992), Haugen and Baker (1991), and Winston (1993).

Investment Style

Investment style is a commonly used term, although it is virtually impossible to identify a consensus meaning for it. Most practitioners agree that investment style describes the types of securities a manager typically selects for his or her portfolio. Others go further and use the term to summarize the manager's methods of portfolio construction.

Definition of Investment Style. At the asset category level, investment style has attained a standard usage, clearly marking the boundaries inside which most managers operate. A domestic common stock manager primarily invests in U.S. common stocks, for example. Within asset categories, however, practitioners are much less in agreement among themselves. Consequently, managers and consultants feel less constrained by the relatively nebulous definitions applied at that level.

Within the domestic equity asset category, practitioners often define investment style qualitatively. In this context, investment style refers to distinctive and continually applied aspects of a manager's investment process. Such terms as *top down, bottom up, quant, growth, value,* and *sector rotator* are often used.

Although these qualitative definitions are useful in many situations, for purposes of analyzing the effects of combining managers' investment styles, we prefer a more rigorous and quantitative definition. In particular, we define a manager's investment style as a set of prominent investment characteristics that the manager's portfolios persistently exhibit. By "prominent investment characteristics," we mean measurable financial attributes of the portfolio that are significantly correlated with its returns.

William Sharpe popularized this approach to style identification. In a widely cited article, Sharpe (1992) applied a factor model to analyze a manager's or fund's returns. The Sharpe methodology defines investment style as the combination of various investable market indexes whose returns statistically explain the manager's or fund's returns. For example, a small-capitalization/growth stock manager is a manager whose returns are predominantly explained by the returns on a combination of indexes representing small-capitalization stocks and growth stocks. More eclectic managers may find their investment styles defined by combinations of market indexes extending across asset categories.

An alternative approach to quantitatively determining a manager's investment style is to use a multifactor model to examine the composition of the manager's past portfolios and the exposures of those portfolios to various factors. The manager's style is then defined as the average exposures to those factors over the observation period. In most cases, the two quantitative style-classification methods will produce similar conclusions. In general, the

10

returns-based analysis is easier to implement whereas the asset-based analysis makes more complete use of available information.

The Importance of Investment Style. Why do plan sponsors and managers feel the need to specify managers' investment styles? The overriding reason is the recognition that investment styles have a significant impact on managers' returns. Figure 1.2 illustrates the performance of four domestic equity "generic" style portfolios (defined in this situation as value, growth, small capitalization, and large capitalization) relative to the S&P 500 for three-year rolling periods. The long-term trends in relative performance are fascinating to observe. Furthermore, the differences in returns among the styles are dramatic; in many three-year periods, the gap between the highest- and lowest-performing styles exceeds 10 percentage points a year.[7]

In the short term, no domestic equity manager could ever hope to overcome these style effects with his or her active-management skills. Thus, plan sponsors desiring to understand the value-added capabilities of their managers must somehow account for the managers' investment styles in their performance evaluations. More importantly from our perspective, if a sponsor inadvertently allocates its assets only to managers using a similar investment style, then the combined return of those managers is likely to differ considerably from the return of the target. Clearly articulating the investment styles of the plan's managers is the key to effectively controlling style risk.

The significance of investment style leads plan sponsors to seek managers who use particular investment styles. The managers, in turn, advertise their investment approaches as encompassing one style or another. Consultants reinforce these practices by compiling manager databases categorized by investment styles and by exhorting managers to remain true to their stated styles. Managers frequently lament the so-called pigeonholing of their investment approaches, but intelligently applied manager style identification does bring an important element of discipline to plan sponsors' investment programs.

Mapping Domestic Equity Investment Styles

Regardless of the approach used to define investment style, the ability to visually convey such definitions enhances the interpretation and control of style risk. One useful method involves mapping a portfolio's factor exposures, as measured by a multifactor risk model, into two dimensions—size and value versus growth.[8]

---

[7] For annual periods, 30+ percentage point differences in the returns on the generic style portfolios have occurred.

[8] The importance of value versus growth and large-cap versus small-cap investment styles received academic recognition with the work of Fama and French (1992). Practitioners, however, had been applying these concepts long before the Fama and French study.

Figure 1.2. Value versus Growth and Large Capitalization versus Small Capitalization Style Returns

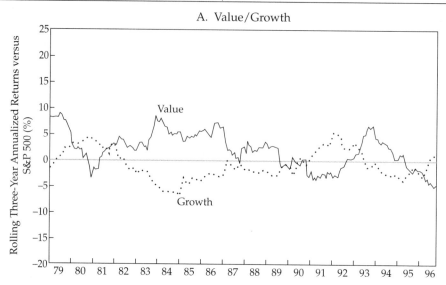

A. Value/Growth

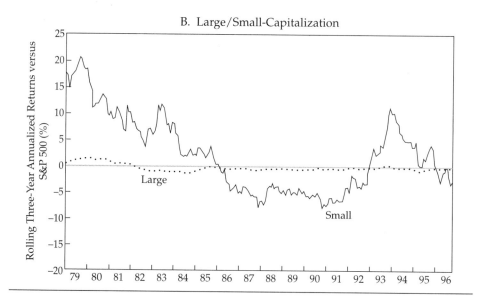

B. Large/Small-Capitalization

The Style-Mapping Process. As described in Tierney and Winston (1991), the style-mapping process begins with four "corner" portfolios, representing four investment styles defined along two dimensions: large-capitalization growth and value and small-capitalization growth and value. The covariances of the corner portfolios are then calculated using the risk model. The corner portfolios serve as numeraires, with their styles defined arbitrarily as ±1 along the two dimensions. Given the composition of a particular portfolio, its covariances with the corner portfolios can be mathematically transformed into a style point expressed two-dimensionally using the ±1 scale.[9]

In style mapping, distance effectively translates into correlation. The closer that two portfolios lie in style space, the more highly correlated are their expected returns. Although the style mapping is not as precise as a full factor model analysis in expressing the covariance between two portfolios, it does have the advantage of being visually appealing and intuitive. We use this style-mapping approach frequently throughout the monograph to illustrate a number of concepts and empirical results.[10]

From a mathematical perspective, the asset-based style-mapping technique and the returns-based method that Sharpe proposed are essentially equivalent. The primary difference lies in the manner in which they estimate covariances between a manager's portfolio and the corner portfolios. The Sharpe style maps use a time series of the manager's returns and the returns on various market indexes; asset-based style maps use a risk model that is applied to a portfolio of securities at a point in time.

The asset-based style maps have the advantage that they do not require a continuous sequence of returns. A few portfolios scattered over time generally provide a clear view of a manager's investment style. Furthermore, the asset-based style maps are not as easily confused by managers who display a "rotating" investment style. Unlike the returns-based style maps, however, the asset-based approach relies on a risk model that effectively captures the sources of return. For certain classes of securities (for example, emerging market stocks), reliable risk models may not be available. Furthermore, even

---

[9]Note that mapping two dimensions requires only three corners because a plane is defined by three points. Analogously, one needs only three legs to secure a table. The fourth leg is unnecessary and adds wobble (uncertainty) to the table. The practical problem of generating a style map with three points instead of four is that long/short exposures occur more frequently as an increased number of portfolios lie outside the region formed by the three corners.

[10]The style-mapping concept can be taken to the level of individual stocks (in essence, a two-factor model). When plotting individual stocks in style space, we found that value stocks outnumber growth stocks and small stocks outnumber large stocks. The dispersion of individual stocks is much greater than that of portfolios but is fairly symmetrical across the mapping space, albeit with a longer tail in the small direction.

a few portfolio asset lists are often more difficult to collect than a series of monthly or quarterly manager returns. Despite these differences, our research has indicated that the two style-mapping methods produce virtually the same results when applied to managers whose primary focus is on stock selection. This observation is comforting, given that most domestic equity managers concentrate on picking individual stocks as opposed to aggressively rotating among sectors or switching between stocks and cash.

Style Dispersion. Using the asset-based style-mapping method with the ±1 scale, Figure 1.3 plots the location of a number of widely recognized domestic equity indexes. Figure 1.4 gives a sense of the wide dispersion of investment styles among domestic equity managers. As of September 30, 1996, the portfolios of 182 domestic equity managers had been plotted in style space relative to the four generic style portfolios. Most of these managers do not hold portfolios similar to the S&P 500, which is also plotted in Figure 1.4 as a reference point. The figure clearly illustrates the inadequacy of attempting to represent manager investment styles with a single broad market index.

Figure 1.3. Style Locations of Various Domestic Equity Market Indexes, September 1996

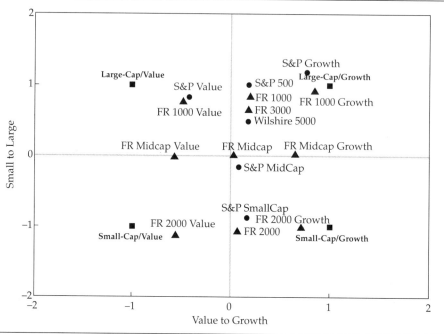

Note: FR = Frank Russell.

Figure 1.4. Style Distributions of Active Managers' Portfolios, September 1996

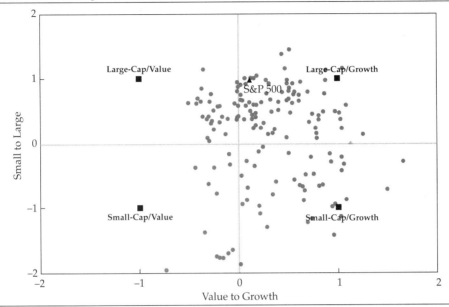

Growth managers, particularly large-cap/growth managers, appear to outnumber value managers. We can only speculate on the reasons for this disparity. We suspect that managers are attracted to growth styles because those styles represent a more glamorous story to sell to prospective clients. Furthermore, growth investing likely presents an exciting career path for analysts and portfolio managers. Attempting to find the next successful biotech company may be more interesting than analyzing the financial prospects for an electric utility company. Also, managers and plan sponsors may fall victim to the fallacy of equating future high earnings growth rates with correspondingly high prospective common stock returns.

Manager Benchmarks

Closely related to the notion of manager investment styles are manager benchmarks. A manager's *benchmark*, formed by a list of securities and associated investment weights, is the tangible expression of the manager's investment style. It serves three primary purposes. First, it formally communicates a manager's investment style both to clients and to decision makers within the manager's organization. A benchmark is a passive representation of the manager's investment process. As such, it delineates the manager's area of expertise by providing a clear picture of the types of securities from which the manager constructs portfolios and the typical investment characteristics of those portfolios. Second, a benchmark is the appropriate standard against which to evaluate the value of a manager's active investment judgments. A valid benchmark reduces the amount of "noise" in the performance-evaluation process, providing a more accurate picture of a manager's investment skill. Third (and, for the purpose of this monograph, most importantly), a benchmark facilitates the allocation of funds to managers within a plan sponsor's investment program so as to regulate the style risk of the total portfolio. By combining its existing (and any prospective) managers' benchmarks, the sponsor can analyze and control the range of performance outcomes (relative to the target) that various allocations to the managers' investment styles will produce.

Properties of a Valid Benchmark. What defines an acceptable benchmark? No simple answer exists, but we contend that a valid benchmark should possess several basic attributes.[11] It should be

- *unambiguous*—the names and weights of securities comprising the benchmark are clearly delineated;
- *investable*—the option is available to forgo active management and simply hold the benchmark;
- *measurable*—the benchmark's return can be readily calculated on a reasonably frequent basis;
- *appropriate*—the benchmark is consistent with the manager's investment style;
- *reflective of current investment opinions*—the manager has current investment knowledge (be it positive, negative, or neutral) regarding the securities that constitute the benchmark;
- *specified in advance*—the benchmark is constructed prior to the start of an evaluation period;
- *accountable*—the manager accepts ownership and accountability for the composition and performance of the benchmark.

Benchmarks failing to possess these attributes compromise the performance-evaluation and risk-control functions for which the benchmarks were created in the first place.

Our experience has been that the most common and serious problems in benchmark design involve investability and advance availability. Both features cut to the heart of the issue of providing a true passive alternative to investing in the manager's actual portfolio. Unless a benchmark offers this alternative, it has little relevance for understanding and evaluating a manager's investment process.

---

[11] For additional discussion of basic benchmark issues, see Bailey, Richards, and Tierney (1988) and Divecha and Grinold (1989).

A manager should be responsible for demonstrating the validity of his or her benchmark. By formally accepting the manager's benchmark, however, the plan sponsor assumes responsibility for the benchmark's performance relative to the target. At the same time, the manager becomes accountable for his or her performance relative to the benchmark.

Subsequently, both the manager and the sponsor must resist the temptation to substitute other performance standards for the benchmark whenever doing so would appear temporarily to serve either party's advantage. For example, managers justifiably complain that their clients often hold them accountable for performance relative to their assigned benchmarks and to the target during periods when the managers' investment styles underperform the target. Conversely, during periods when they have failed to add value to their assigned benchmarks, managers are often guilty of referencing various irrelevant performance bogeys that they happened to have outperformed. Pursuing these "red herrings" is ultimately counterproductive. Managers and plan sponsors are better served in the long run if they devote their efforts to developing benchmarks that possess the attributes just described.

Approaches to Building Manager Benchmarks. Practitioners currently use three primary approaches to constructing benchmarks for domestic equity managers: They are either assignment based, returns based, or asset based.

▪ *Assignment-based benchmarks.* An assignment-based benchmark involves placing a manager in one of several predetermined style categories. Domestic equity managers might be assigned to the generic style indexes to which their portfolios are most closely aligned. For example, returning to Figure 1.3, a manager whose portfolios plot in the lower left quadrant would be assigned a small-cap/value index as the benchmark.

The assignment-based approach has the advantage of simplicity and ease of implementation. Consequently, it has been highly popular among performance-evaluation consultants. The primary drawback of this approach, however, stems from its simplicity. It ignores subtle but critical information about unique elements of managers' investment styles. For example, large-cap/growth managers, whom many practitioners tend to view as a fairly homogenous group, can vary significantly in the types of portfolios they own. The reason is fundamental differences in how they go about determining attractive investments. Figure 1.5 plots monthly portfolios over the past five years for two well-known large-cap/growth managers. In style space, the distance between these two managers is considerable and translates into

Figure 1.5. Large-Cap/Growth Managers' Style Locations, Five Years Ending September 1996

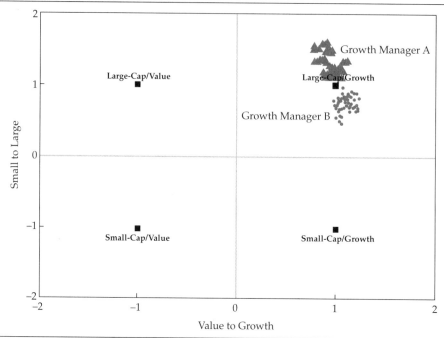

potentially large deviations in performance.[12] But the assignment-based approach would treat these managers as if they pursued the same style.

■ *Returns-based benchmarks.* A returns-based benchmark uses the Sharpe style-classification methodology. The combination of style indexes that best explains the manager's set of historical investment returns is computed. That combination of indexes is then converted into a benchmark by simply creating a single portfolio composed of all securities held in the various indexes, with weights determined by the securities' positions in their respective indexes and the indexes' allocations in the benchmark.

The returns-based approach incorporates considerably more information about the manager's investment style than does the assignment-based approach. Historical returns have been shown to be efficient predictors of investment style. Requiring only a set of past returns for the manager and the

---

[12]We obtained custom benchmarks for these two managers that were designed to reflect each manager's individual investment style. For the five-year period ending in third-quarter 1996, Manager A's benchmark returned 15.2 percent annually and Manager B's benchmark produced a 17.9 percent annual return. The Russell 1000 Growth Index, a likely assignment-based benchmark for both managers, generated a 14.8 percent annual return during that period.

candidate style indexes, along with widely available computer software, the returns-based approach also has the advantage of ease of application. As a result, returns-based benchmarks have rapidly gained adherents, particularly among those plan sponsors that prefer to (or have no choice but to) build benchmarks without the participation of their managers.

The drawbacks of the returns-based approach lie both in its reliance on historical returns to compute the appropriate combination of style indexes and in the composition of the style indexes themselves. The method assumes a stability in investment style that may not be present, particularly in the case of managers who exhibit a "rotational" investment style or who have somehow fundamentally altered their investment processes. Furthermore, it ignores subtle aspects of the manager's investment process that can be obtained only through direct discussion with the manager. Moreover, combining style indexes may force securities into the manager's benchmark for which he or she has no current research coverage and at weights that may be disproportionate to the securities' actual importance in the manager's investment process.

If the benchmark builder blindly follows a set of prescribed procedures, the returns-based approach can be victimized by spurious correlations. That is, the list of candidate indexes may include entire asset classes in which the manager has absolutely no investment expertise or past involvement. For example, a domestic equity manager's returns may indicate a modest correlation with an index of international fixed-income securities. Including such an index in the domestic equity manager's benchmark may lead to the uncomfortable situation in which the manager underperforms or outperforms the benchmark solely by not owning any international fixed-income assets.

■ *Asset-based benchmarks.* The asset-based approach is the most comprehensive of the three benchmark-building approaches. It involves a thorough "audit" of the manager's investment process.[13] The goal of that audit is to create a custom list of assets and associated weights based on the benchmark builder's quantitative and qualitative interpretation of the manager's investment style.

The primary advantage of the asset-based approach is its use of all available information relevant to the manager's investment process, including past returns, past security holdings, promotional literature provided by the manager, and information gleaned from discussions with the manager. Rather than rely on the composition and weighting scheme of arbitrarily defined

---

[13]The process of building an asset-based benchmark is described in Bailey, Richards, and Tierney (1990).

market indexes to determine the holdings of the benchmark, the asset-based approach develops security holdings designed to reflect that manager's investment style on an *ex ante* basis, as opposed to the *ex post* basis of the returns-based approach.[14]

The main drawback of the asset-based approach is the significant effort involved. A considerable amount of data must be collected and reviewed. Successful application requires data analysis expertise and customized computer software. Furthermore, the manager must be intimately involved in designing the benchmark and must be willing to discuss basic (although not proprietary) elements of his or her investment process. Generally, the asset-based approach requires considerably more time and expense than the returns-based approach.

Cash in Manager Benchmarks. Practitioners generally acknowledge that almost all domestic equity managers permanently invest a portion of their portfolios in various high-quality, short-term fixed-income investments that we will generically call "cash." These cash positions have nothing to do with the managers' views on the relative value of the domestic equity market. Rather, they usually result from sources such as the following:

- *Frictions in the trading process and income accruals.* The timing of sales does not always match the timing of purchases. Therefore, managers tend to keep some cash to guard against temporarily overdrawing their available funds. Furthermore, dividend income earned but not yet paid goes on the books as cash.
- *"Dry powder" for new investment ideas.* Managers wish to avoid having to sell existing holdings when they come across attractive investment ideas. Keeping a cash reserve avoids a forced sale of portfolio holdings.
- *Volatility dampening.* Managers may deliberately hold equity investments with higher levels of systematic risk than they would normally feel comfortable with. They dilute that excess risk with cash.

The size of these permanent cash positions varies among domestic equity managers. Permanent cash levels in the range of 0.5–10.0 percent are common. Some managers will maintain permanent cash allocations as high as 20–30 percent. Given the ubiquitous nature of cash in managers' portfolios, it

---

[14]This distinction between *ex ante* and *ex post* can be important in benchmark building. Consider an investment management firm that has recently lost its chemicals analyst. As a result, the firm no longer covers the chemicals industry and would thus not own chemical company stocks. Therefore, those stocks should be removed from the manager's benchmark until a new chemicals analyst is hired and the manager develops informed opinions about chemical company stocks. A benchmark-building analysis performed on an *ex ante* basis would account for this change, but an *ex post* analysis would not.

would seem only natural that cash would play a prominent role in manager benchmarks.

The idea of benchmark cash has sparked considerable controversy. Many plan sponsors that otherwise strongly endorse the use of benchmarks designed to reflect managers' unique investment styles vehemently oppose including cash in those benchmarks. Their primary contention is that cash is an unproductive asset for domestic equity managers. Consequently, any cash those managers hold should be viewed as an active strategy. We disagree with this viewpoint. Managers' permanent cash positions represent distinguishing characteristics of their investment styles. Therefore, those cash positions should be incorporated in their benchmarks, as should any other security that the manager normally holds. Furthermore, our research indicates that the inclusion of cash in manager benchmarks greatly enhances the benchmarks' ability to pass reasonable quality tests.

Investment Skill

Investment skill is the ability to outperform an appropriate benchmark consistently over time. We refer to a manager's excess returns relative to his or her benchmark as *active-management returns* or the *value of active management (VAM)*.[15] No manager is omniscient; therefore, managers' value-added returns will be positive in some periods and negative in others. Although a skillful manager should perform well in any given period, the manager's actual performance will vary over time. Even sophisticated investors tend to focus on expected value-added returns and ignore value-added uncertainty. In their presentations, domestic equity managers often claim that they will beat their benchmarks by, say, 3–10 percent a year. They virtually never disclose (nor do their clients prompt them to disclose) that the expected variability (standard deviation) of those superior returns might range from 2 percent to 12 percent a year.

Although all active managers will exhibit some variability in their realized value-added returns, skillful managers, on average, will produce greater positive value added relative to the variability of their active-management results than will their less-talented peers. The ratio of value-added returns to the variability of those returns (on either an *ex post* or *ex ante* basis) is referred to as the *information ratio* (IR);[16] that is,

$$IR = \frac{VAM}{\sigma_{VAM}}.$$

---

[15] A manager's VAM is also referred to as the manager's alpha or risk-adjusted return.
[16] The information ratio is discussed at length in Grinold (1989) and Sharpe (1994).

The information ratio is the appropriate measure of a manager's skill. Plan sponsors should prefer managers who generate high and/or consistent portfolio returns relative to the returns of the managers' respective benchmarks.

The inherently volatile nature of investment performance makes the identification of investment skill based solely on past performance a statistically difficult exercise. In the uncertain world of investment management, luck often masquerades as skill and skill is frequently overwhelmed by random events. Consider the following example. We identify a superior manager who we know in advance will, on average, beat his or her benchmark by 2 percent annually. The variability of that expected value-added return is 5 percent a year. Our hypothetical manager has an *ex ante* information ratio of 0.40 (2 percent divided by 5 percent), which in our experience is a very high number, hence our assertion that the manager is skillful. Table 1.2 shows the probability that managers with given information ratios will outperform their benchmarks over various evaluation periods.

We have preordained that, in the long run, our skillful manager will outperform less-proficient managers. Perhaps surprisingly, Table 1.2 indicates that the skillful manager has a one-in-four chance of underperforming his or her benchmark over a period as long as three years. Remember, we have defined the manager in advance to be a superior manager. Other value-added managers with less skill than this manager will have even greater chances of underperforming their benchmarks over typical evaluation periods.

The difficulty of identifying investment skill based on past performance makes it critical to distinguish between the returns derived from *investment*

Table 1.2. Probability of a Manager Outperforming a Benchmark, Given Various Levels of Investment Skill

Measurement Period (years)	Information Ratio					
	0.2	0.3	0.4	0.67	0.8	1.0
0.5	55.6%	58.4%	61.1%	68.1%	71.4%	76.0%
1.0	57.9	61.8	65.5	74.7	78.8	84.0
3.0	63.8	69.8	75.6	87.6	91.7	95.8
5.0	67.3	74.9	81.5	93.2	96.3	98.7
10.0	73.6	82.9	89.7	98.3	99.4	99.9
20.0	81.7	91.0	96.3	99.9	99.9	99.9

style and the returns derived from *investment skill*.[17] The situation is analogous to the difference between one-time and sustainable corporate earnings. Investment style is not proprietary. By definition, it can be replicated by a benchmark. The benchmark is based on publicly available information about the manager's investment process that is known in advance of an evaluation period. Therefore, just as extraordinary sources of corporate earnings should not be expected to repeat regularly, a particular investment style should not be expected to outperform the target persistently on a risk-adjusted basis. Investment skill, on the other hand, represents the unique aspects of a manager's investment process. Just as sustainable corporate earnings can be counted on to recur predictably, investment skill should be expected to produce positive results both in markets that are relatively favorable and in markets that are unfavorable for the manager's investment style.[18]

Realistically, superior domestic equity managers can be expected to outperform their benchmarks (on a net-of-fee basis) by at most 100 to 200 basis points (bps) a year. As we have discussed, however, differences between domestic equity generic style returns can exceed 3,000 bps a year. Consequently, investment style tends to obscure the abilities of even the most skillful managers, making the plan sponsor's task of identifying superior managers extremely difficult. Appropriate design of manager benchmarks permits a performance evaluator to strip away the investment style elements of returns, leaving the contributions of investment skill (and luck) for further analysis.

Some Simple Portfolio-Management Algebra

At this point, we can begin to apply a simple mathematical framework to the concepts we have discussed. Start with the identity of an investment manager's portfolio:[19]

$$P = P. \tag{1.1}$$

Now, consider an appropriately selected benchmark, B. Adding and subtracting B from the right-hand side of Equation 1.1 gives

$$P = B + (P - B). \tag{1.2}$$

---

[17] Kritzman (1986) addresses the subject of separating investment skill from investment style.
[18] In mathematical terms, the manager's value-added process is orthogonal to the manager's investment style.
[19] Equation 1.1 and the various equations that follow can be thought of as referring to returns or to security holdings, as the context of the discussion dictates.

If we define the manager's active investment judgments, A, as being the difference between the manager's portfolio, P, and the benchmark, B, so that $A = P - B$, then Equation 1.2 becomes

$$P = B + A. \tag{1.3}$$

Equation 1.3 states that a manager's portfolio can be partitioned into two components: the manager's benchmark (or investment style) and the manager's active-management decisions (or investment skill).

The active-management component is composed of a set of long, short, and zero positions relative to the benchmark. That is, the manager believes that some securities are undervalued and thus holds them in portions greater than their representation in the benchmark. Conversely, the manager believes that other securities are overvalued or fairly valued. He or she holds those securities in proportions less than or equal to, respectively, their positions in the benchmark. In total, the weights of all securities in A must sum to zero. Thus, we refer to A as a *hedge portfolio*.[20]

If we now introduce an asset category target, T, and add and subtract it from the right-hand side of Equation 1.3, then we have

$$P = T + (B - T) + A. \tag{1.4}$$

The manager's portfolio can be viewed as being composed of a systematic component, T, a component that represents how the manager's style differs from the target, $B - T$, and the active-management component, A. All managers operating within the asset category are exposed to the systematic source of returns, as reflected in T. Managers' unique investment styles, however, as represented by their benchmarks, determine their biases relative to the target. The plan sponsor pays the manager to take active bets that both parties anticipate will add value to the benchmark's results, as indicated by A.

Benchmark Orthogonality Properties

The disaggregation of the manager's portfolio in Equations 1.3 and 1.4 leads directly to two properties of a valid benchmark, called benchmark orthogonality properties:

- The performance of the value-added component, A, should be uncorrelated with the performance of the benchmark, B. That is, $\text{Cov}(A,B) = 0$.
- The performance of the value-added component, A, should be uncorrelated with the performance of the asset category target, T; that is, $\text{Cov}(A,T) = 0$.

---

[20]Managers' benchmarks are composed of hundreds of securities. Yet, most active domestic equity managers own 30 to 70 stocks in their portfolios. Those stocks not owned represent short positions in the active-management components of the managers' portfolios.

Both benchmark orthogonality properties arise from common sense and are symmetrical. If the benchmark has adequately captured the manager's investment style, then the manager's performance relative to that benchmark should be unrelated to how either the manager's investment style or the target performs.

A benchmark is created based on publicly available information regarding a manager's investment process. Consequently, we should expect that investing passively in the benchmark offers only the expectation of a zero risk-adjusted return.[21] Given this no-value condition of the benchmark, if we take the return expectations, denoted E, of the three components of Equation 1.4, then $E(B - T) = 0$ and $E(P) = E(T) + E(A)$. Rearranging terms gives

$$E(A) = E(P) - E(T). \tag{1.5}$$

Despite the increased recognition of the importance of investment styles on manager performance, many plan sponsors and consultants remain interested in evaluating a manager's results relative to a target. As Equation 1.5 shows, however, the only way the manager can expect to outperform the plan sponsor's target on a risk-adjusted basis is if the manager expects to outperform the benchmark; that is, $E(A) > 0$.

Implications of Benchmark Orthogonality. The volatility of the manager's returns relative to those of the target is found by moving T to the left-hand side of Equation 1.4 and taking the variance on both sides; that is,

$$\mathrm{Var}(P - T) = \mathrm{Var}[(B - T) + A]$$
$$= \mathrm{Var}(B - T) + \mathrm{Var}(A) + 2\mathrm{Cov}[(B - T), A].$$

From the benchmark orthogonality properties, we know that $\mathrm{Cov}[(B - T), A] = 0$. Therefore,

$$\mathrm{Var}(P - T) = \mathrm{Var}(B - T) + \mathrm{Var}(A). \tag{1.6}$$

Because $\mathrm{Var}(B - T) \geq 0$, Equation 1.6 demonstrates that the portfolio's returns relative to the target can be no less variable than the portfolio's returns relative to the benchmark, despite the fact that they both have the same return expectation. This fact brings us back to the issue of separating manager skill from investment style. Investment skill is more readily discernible when evaluated relative to a valid benchmark than to the asset category target because the benchmark explicitly accounts for the impact of the manager's investment style on performance.

---

[21] In our simple portfolio algebra, we are implicitly assuming that all of the elements, P, B, A, and T, have the same level of systematic risk or that the return expectations have included an adjustment for risk.

The benefits of examining a manager's performance relative to a valid benchmark instead of the target are further highlighted if we refer back to the information ratio. On an *ex ante* basis, let Z represent the difference between a portfolio's return and the return on an investable alternative portfolio. Then,

$$IR(Z) = \frac{E(Z)}{\sqrt{Var(Z)}}.$$

From Equations 1.5 and 1.6, it must be true that

$$IR(A) \geq IR(P - T).$$

Therefore, if we are evaluating a manager's investment skill, as represented by the manager's information ratio, our test can never be less exact, and likely will be more exact, than using returns compared against a properly constructed benchmark rather than returns compared against the target.

This point is illustrated in Figure 1.6. The upper panel presents two hypothetical return distributions, one associated with a manager's benchmark return relative to the target and the other corresponding to the manager's portfolio return relative to the benchmark. Both distributions have the same standard deviation of 5 percent, but the benchmark-minus-target distribution has an expected value of zero and the portfolio-minus-benchmark distribution has an expected value of 2 percent. The lower panel of Figure 1.6 shows the distribution of the manager's portfolio returns relative to the target. Notice that the distribution of these returns is broader than either of the two distributions in the upper panel of Figure 1.6 (in fact, the standard deviation is 7.1 percent, or $\sqrt{2} \times 5.0$ percent), but it remains centered at 2.0 percent.

The areas to the left of zero on the horizontal axes in Figure 1.6 represent the probability of the manager underperforming the benchmark and the target, respectively. As can be seen, the probability of the manager underperforming the target is greater than that of underperforming the benchmark, despite the manager's "true" skill being indifferent to the performance standard applied. Comparing the manager's performance with that of the target injects noise into the evaluation process, which tends to obscure investment skill.

Benchmark Misfit

Up until this point, we have made many references to the difference between a manager's benchmark and the target without giving this difference a formal name. Henceforth, we will call that difference benchmark misfit, or simply *misfit*. (A synonymous term practitioners sometimes use is *style bias*.) Misfit implies that in some way the benchmark does not match, or fit, the target.

©The Research Foundation of the ICFA

Figure 1.6. Relative Return Distributions

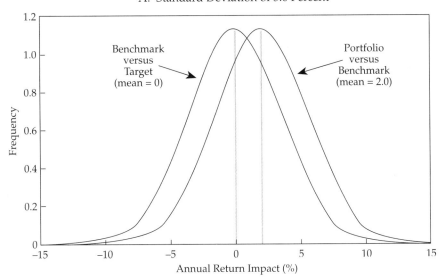

A. Standard Deviation of 5.0 Percent

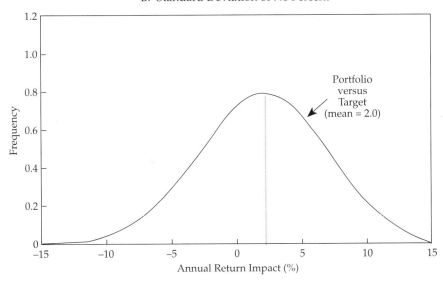

B. Standard Deviation of 7.1 Percent

Definition of Misfit. If the benchmark and target are properly specified as unambiguous, investable portfolios, then we can calculate misfit on a security-by-security basis, thereby creating a misfit portfolio. This misfit portfolio will contain both long and short positions. Consider the simple example shown in Table 1.3. The table shows the holdings of the benchmark, the target, and the misfit portfolio, all stated in percentage terms. For example, Security 1 is held in the benchmark at a 21 percent position, but it constitutes only 13 percent of the target. As a result, the misfit portfolio contains a positive 8 percent position in Security 1; the manager's investment style emphasizes Security 1 relative to the plan sponsor's target.

The weights of the securities in either the benchmark or the target, of course, must sum to 100 percent. The weights of the misfit portfolio's securities, however, must sum to zero because the long positions exactly offset the short positions. (Thus, the misfit portfolio is a hedge portfolio, as is the active-management component of a manager's portfolio.) If the manager's benchmark overweights a particular security relative to the target, then the benchmark must necessarily underweight one or more other securities.

Figure 1.7 illustrates the misfit concept. Manager A's benchmark is placed in style space relative to a particular plan sponsor's target. Because the two portfolios are separated from one another, they can be expected to produce different returns in any given measurement period.

Misfit Return. In any given period, misfit return for an individual manager, or a group of managers, is likely to be some nonzero value. In fact, misfit return, in many cases, will exceed the value-added return a manager or a group

---

Table 1.3. Example of a Misfit Portfolio

Security	Benchmark Holdings	Asset Category Target Holdings	Misfit Portfolio Holdings (% points)
1	21.0%	13.0%	+8.0
2	0.0	9.0	−9.0
3	24.0	15.0	+9.0
4	30.0	6.0	+24.0
5	0.0	5.0	−5.0
6	0.0	16.0	−16.0
7	0.0	8.0	−8.0
8	8.0	11.0	−3.0
9	0.0	10.0	−10.0
10	17.0	7.0	+10.0
Total	100.0%	100.0%	0.0

Figure 1.7. The Misfit Concept

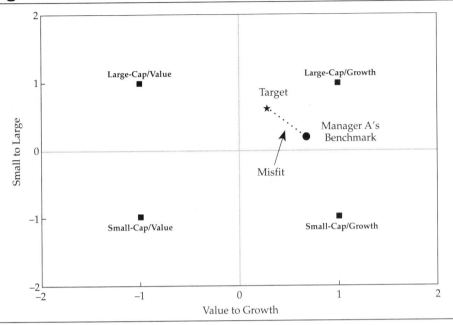

of managers produces. Some plan sponsors believe that they can anticipate how managers' investment styles will perform in the near term relative to their targets and will adjust their managers' allocations accordingly. Nevertheless, a plan sponsor should not expect that a manager's benchmark (or the aggregate benchmark of the managers) will systematically outperform the target or vice versa in the long run on a risk-adjusted basis. Indeed, if such an expectation exists, the sponsor has misspecified the target. Therefore, we operate under the assumption that the expected risk-adjusted misfit return is zero.

Misfit Risk. The variability of misfit return is always non-negative. We refer to this variability as *misfit risk*. It too can be measured for an individual manager or a group of managers. Furthermore, it can be contrasted with active-management risk, or the variability of value-added returns.

Our experience has been that for domestic equity programs, on average, $\text{Var}(B - T) \cong \text{Var}(A)$. In other words, if we combine all of a plan sponsor's domestic equity managers into one portfolio, the variability of the combined managers' benchmark returns relative to the target's return is typically at least as volatile as the combined active-management returns generated by the managers. For many plan sponsors, the practical implication is that they expose themselves to as much variability in returns from a risk source with zero expected return as they do from a risk source anticipated to enhance the performance of the investment program.

Capital market theory teaches that unproductive risk should be avoided. A plan sponsor hires active managers with the expectation that the value-added returns they produce will more than compensate for the active-management risk they impose on the investment program. Because a sponsor has no expectation of risk-adjusted gain by incurring misfit risk, misfit-return volatility can only serve to reduce the sponsor's utility. We conclude that the thoughtful sponsor should adopt investment policies that minimize the level of the misfit present in the plan's investment program up to the point at which the costs of those minimization efforts equal the benefits.

The Cost of Misfit Risk

To the extent that misfit risk reduces a plan sponsor's utility, that reduction implies a cost. Appendix A presents an expression for the cost of misfit risk. Specifically, we show that for a typical investment program, the cost is at least

$$\left[1 + \frac{\text{Var}(B-T)}{\text{Var}(T)}\right]^{\frac{1}{2}} - 1 \times E(T-F), \tag{1.7}$$

where $E(T-F)$ is the expected return premium of the target over the risk-free asset.

The intuition underlying this expression is straightforward. If the misfit risk is zero (i.e., $\text{Var}[B-T] = 0$), then its cost is zero. To the extent that the benchmark deviates from the target, misfit risk results, which adds to the total risk of the plan sponsor's portfolio. We can approximate that incremental risk by appropriately leveraging the target; that is, we can calculate the increase in the target's beta that would produce a level of risk commensurate with that added by the misfit. We can then compute the "cost" of that increased beta by appealing to the CAPM. It will give us the increased expected return associated with the increase in beta. This cost can be interpreted as the extra expected return required to compensate the plan sponsor for taking on the additional risk caused by misfit.

To give some life to this analysis, we can attach some numbers to Expression 1.7 and derive an estimated domestic equity misfit cost for a hypothetical plan sponsor. Assume that the expected return of the target over the risk-free rate is 9 percent, the variance of that return is 289 (a 17 percent standard deviation squared), and the variance of the plan sponsor's misfit return is 9 (a 3 percent standard deviation squared). Therefore, the cost of misfit is at least

$$\left(1 + \frac{9}{289}\right)^{\frac{1}{2}} - 1 \times 9 = 0.139 \text{ percent.}$$

For a $1 billion domestic equity portfolio, an annual misfit cost of 13.9 bps translates into $1.39 million a year of additional investment performance required to compensate for the added risk caused by the managers' investment styles, in aggregate, being out of alignment with the target.

The Magnitude of Misfit Risk

How large is the misfit risk to which plan sponsors are exposed? That question is difficult to answer empirically. Measuring misfit risk involves, among other things, establishing valid benchmarks for every one of the plan sponsor's managers within the asset category under consideration, assigning policy allocations to each of the managers, and selecting an appropriate target. To date, only a few plan sponsors have implemented the disciplined and sophisticated procedures necessary for such a detailed analysis. Despite these challenges, we have been able to accumulate what we believe to be a robust set of domestic equity misfit data for a reasonably large group of plan sponsors.

Methodology. We collected data on the active-management components of 12 plan sponsors' domestic equity programs. All of the programs use a multiple-active-manager structure, with the number of active managers ranging from a low of 4 to a high of 15. Table 1.4 lists the plan sponsors included in the study (coded to disguise their identities) and the corresponding sizes of their actively managed domestic equity assets. In total, those assets exceed $18 billion.

Table 1.4. Plan Sponsor Forecast Active-Management and Misfit Risk, June 1996

Plan Sponsor	Active Domestic Equity Assets ($ millions)	Active-Management Risk	Misfit Risk	Ratio of Active-Management Risk to Misfit Risk
Bronze	$ 454.2	3.53%	1.22%	2.89
Coral	231.8	1.82	1.61	1.13
Diamond	751.2	2.18	3.50	0.62
Emerald	5,846.6	1.37	1.00	1.37
Gold	285.5	1.76	0.93	1.89
Ivory	5,836.4	1.20	1.86	0.65
Opal	127.5	2.06	2.49	0.83
Platinum	107.2	3.13	4.63	0.68
Ruby	897.2	2.28	3.47	0.66
Sapphire	3,220.1	1.98	1.12	1.77
Topaz	676.1	2.09	0.88	2.37
Uranium	193.8	2.13	2.20	0.97

Our measurements of the misfit and active-management risks present in the plan sponsors' investment programs were centered on June 30, 1996. (To confirm the general consistency of our results, we also examined the same investment programs on December 31, 1995. Because the conclusions drawn from those data were not materially different, we report only the results based on the latest available data.) In several cases in which our data ended prior to this date, we used the most recent information.

For each plan sponsor, our initial step entailed collecting asset lists for the target, as well as all of the plan's actual portfolios and benchmarks for the sponsor's active equity managers. We then identified the policy allocations assigned to each manager. With this information, we aggregated the managers' actual portfolios and their benchmarks.

A plan sponsor's aggregate actual portfolio was created by simply adding together all the security positions in all of its managers' portfolios. The aggregate manager benchmark was created by multiplying the security percentage positions in each manager's benchmark by the manager's policy allocation and then summing across all managers. In creating the aggregate actual and benchmark portfolios, we included passively managed portfolios not indexed to the target. For example, if a sponsor's domestic equity target was the S&P 500, then a Russell-2000-indexed portfolio was included in the aggregate actual portfolio and aggregate manager benchmark, but an S&P-500-indexed portfolio was not. Our rationale for this procedure was that we wished to examine the elements of the sponsors' investment programs that contribute to misfit. Portfolios indexed to the target are neutral in terms of their misfit contribution, but passive portfolios invested in a nontarget market index produce a misfit exposure.

For analyzing the misfit risk of the plan sponsors' investment programs, two alternative approaches were open to us. We could have investigated the *historical* active-management and misfit risk those programs experienced. That approach, however, would have greatly exacerbated the data collection problems. It would have required us to obtain benchmark and actual portfolio return information for a large number of managers for a long enough time period to establish statistical reliability. The second alternative was to apply a commercially available multifactor risk model to compute the *forecast* misfit risk, active-management risk, and total volatility of the domestic equity programs as of the end of second-quarter 1996. We found this approach to be much more tractable because it required data collection on only one date as opposed to building a time series of return data. Furthermore, because the essence of misfit risk control is to be able to predict risk and then establish that the out-of-sample outcome volatility is consistent with the forecast risk, the risk model approach seemed particularly appropriate.[22]

Results. We hypothesized that because active-management risk is intended and misfit risk is not, plan sponsors would seek to maintain high levels of the former relative to the latter. Our results, however, shown in Table 1.4, do not indicate that this group of plan sponsors conformed to our expectations. (All risk figures are reported as annualized standard deviations.)

Contrary to our hypothesis, the predicted misfit risk incurred by 6 of the 12 plan sponsors was greater than their predicted active-management risk (as indicated by the ratio of active-management risk to misfit risk, which was less than 1.00). In fact, the ratio of the average active-management risk to average misfit risk was 1.02, and the median ratio was 1.05. Consequently, approximately half of the forecast return volatility of the active-management components of these domestic equity programs can be traced to their misfit risk, as opposed to the active-management risk their managers assumed.

As a rule, we prefer to see domestic equity misfit risk of less than 1 percent and a ratio of active-management risk to misfit risk of at least 2 or 3. Without such relative risk exposures, the biggest decision affecting the performance of a plan sponsor's active-management program becomes the structuring of the managers' investment styles rather than the managers' investment decisions within those styles. The benefits of any successful active-management program can easily be lost in the noise of misfit.

Inspection of Table 1.4 reveals that only plan sponsors Bronze, Gold, Sapphire, and Topaz come close to meeting this rule of thumb. The other 75 percent of the plan sponsors should implement remedial action to control misfit risk, both in an absolute sense and relative to the level of active-management risk.

We conclude that domestic equity misfit risk is a problem of sufficient magnitude to warrant the attention of plan sponsors, although our results probably understate the level of misfit risk present in most plan sponsors' domestic equity investment programs. Selection bias was a problem in this study. The plan sponsors involved have adopted well-defined investment policies, a process that, at a minimum, acquaints them with the misfit concept. Therefore, their hiring of (and allocation to) investment managers likely reflects at least some attempt to balance investment styles to limit misfit. We anticipate that if we were able to sample plan sponsors randomly, we would

---

[22] Our experience is that multifactor risk models do an adequate job of predicting risks at the portfolio level. Out-of-sample standard deviations usually track within ±20 percent of the predicted values.

find the ratio of active-management risk to misfit risk to be considerably lower than what we found for the 12 plan sponsors in this study.

International Equity Misfit. We strongly suspect that misfit is an even more pervasive problem in plan sponsors' international equity programs than it is in their domestic equity programs. Unfortunately, at this time, the data to conduct a study of international equity programs are virtually impossible to collect. Most plan sponsors select the Morgan Stanley Capital International Europe/Australia/Far East (EAFE) Index as their international equity target. Yet practitioners know full well that few active international equity managers hold portfolios that resemble EAFE's composition. The prime example (but not the only one) is that the Japanese market's weighting in EAFE persistently exceeds the total Japanese stock weightings in the vast majority of active international equity managers' portfolios. This seemingly permanent under-weighting of Japanese stocks persists even when these managers claim that they find the relative valuation of the Japanese market to be attractive.

Such investment style issues should be captured in the international equity managers' benchmarks. Most plan sponsors, however, have been content to use their EAFE asset category target as the universal benchmark for their international equity managers. (This situation is no different—and no less inappropriate—than using the S&P 500 as the benchmark for all of a sponsor's domestic equity managers.) Two casualties of this procedure are that international equity managers' unique investment styles remain obscured and that the misfit problem goes undetected. Although we have little in the way of empirical evidence to offer on the subject, we would not be surprised if international equity misfit risk for large plan sponsors ran in the range of 3–6 percent, as opposed to the 1–4 percent for domestic equity misfit risk.

2. Alternative Approaches to Misfit Control

Plan sponsors can pursue a wide array of strategies to limit misfit—strategies that vary in complexity and effectiveness. A plan sponsor's own unique circumstances will determine which approach is best for it.

To highlight the critical issues involved in choosing an approach, we will examine a hypothetical plan sponsor with a simple multiple-manager investment structure. This sponsor has retained three domestic equity managers and assigned specific allocations of the total investment program to each of them. All of the managers have developed benchmarks that accurately reflect their investment styles. The positions of those benchmarks in style space are shown in Figure 2.1.

As indicated by the benchmarks' different locations on the style map, the managers' benchmarks have risk exposures that differ materially from the target. As a result, each manager exhibits considerable misfit. How should the plan sponsor respond to this situation?

Solution 1: Ignore the Problem

Certainly, the easiest approach to dealing with the misfit problem is to ignore it. In this base-case solution, the plan sponsor does not understand the concepts of investment style or misfit; managers are hired to "beat the market." Consequently, the sponsor assigns each manager the target as his or her benchmark. With a stroke of the pen, misfit is eliminated. Viewed in the context of our discussion, this approach may seem hopelessly naive. Consider, however, how many sponsors insist on using the S&P 500 Index as the universal benchmark for all of their domestic equity managers.

In various aspects of life, ignorance may be bliss, but in the world of investments, it rarely is. Ignoring misfit does not make it go away. Unexpectedly large and negative misfit returns will still appear on occasion to bedevil the plan sponsor's investment program. Although such negative misfit returns may be offset by positive misfit returns over the long term, Figure 1.2 indicates that the "long term" may be very long indeed. The drawn-out bear market for small-cap/growth stocks that many sponsors suffered through in the mid- and late 1980s amply demonstrates the folly of failing to comprehend the ramifications of misfit risk.

Figure 2.1. A Simple Multiple-Manager Alignment

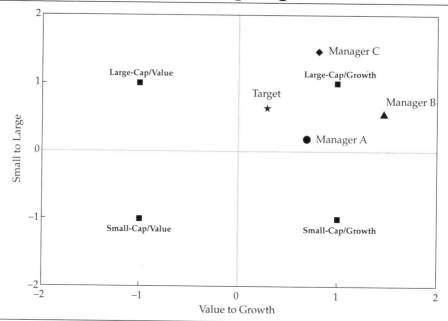

Solution 2: Blame the Managers

A plan sponsor may recognize the presence of misfit but expect (hope?) that its investment managers will overcome the problem through their active-management skills. As in Solution 1, the sponsor assigns all of its managers the target as their benchmarks. When poor markets occur for a particular manager's investment style, the sponsor anticipates that the manager will generate sufficiently large value-added returns to outweigh the negative effects of an out-of-favor investment style. Given the overwhelming size of style returns relative to active-management returns, however, we know that such expectations are unrealistic.

Inevitably, the managers experience periods of significant underperformance. The plan sponsor then chastises the poorly performing managers for their inability to beat the target/benchmark, perhaps dismissing one or more of them as punishment or as a statement to the remaining managers that poor performance (relative to the target) will not be tolerated. Such actions may satisfy the desire of plan trustees to hold someone responsible for the investment program's inability to outperform the target. But the sponsor has not actually solved the misfit problem; in fact, the sponsor has created an unproductive investment environment: Active managers, regardless of their skill, will be hired and fired in a seemingly endless cycle, thereby burdening the investment program with high manager turnover and the attendant transition costs. The problem, of course, lies with the sponsor, not with the active managers.

Solution 3: Transport Alpha for Individual Managers

The growth of over-the-counter swap markets has been one of the more fascinating financial developments of the 1990s. The return on virtually any identifiable portfolio can now be swapped for the return on another portfolio. One possible solution to the misfit problem, therefore, is to exchange the return on each manager's benchmark for the return on the target.

Consider Equation 1.4 again: $P = T + (B - T) + A$. For each manager, the plan sponsor prefers that

$$P = T + A. \tag{2.1}$$

That is, the sponsor desires that each manager's return simply be that of the target plus the manager's active-management return.

Managers hamper achievement of this objective by exhibiting misfit relative to the target $(B - T \neq 0)$. Suppose, however, that the plan sponsor could add T and subtract B from the right-hand side of Equation 1.4. The sponsor could do this by swapping the manager's benchmark return for the return on the target; that is,

$$\begin{aligned} P &= T + (B - T) + A + (T - B) \\ &= T + A. \end{aligned} \tag{2.2}$$

Because Equation 2.2 reduces to Equation 2.1, the result is that the manager delivers the target's returns plus his or her active-management returns.

Conceptually, initiating a swap of each manager's benchmark return for the return on the target resolves the misfit problem. In practice, however, this solution is likely to have a high cost. Market makers, of course, charge a fee to carry out swaps. The more exotic the swap, the greater the fee, because the market maker's hedging risk increases. The cost of implementing swaps for managers with benchmarks that are very dissimilar to the target is likely to be prohibitively expensive.

Just as important, the cost of this solution is exacerbated by treating each manager as an individual misfit problem. When considered in aggregate, the misfits of a plan sponsor's managers often offset one another because diversification of managers' investment styles mitigates the misfit problem. For example, in Figure 2.1, the small-cap bias of Manager A relative to the target is offset by the large-cap bias of Manager C. Swapping Manager A's and Manager C's benchmark returns for the return of the target is essentially unnecessary along the small–large dimension. The message is this: *Investment style and investment skill should be evaluated and controlled from an aggregate portfolio perspective.*

With that principle in mind, consider the individual managers' benchmarks and the aggregate of their benchmarks shown in Figure 2.2. The aggregate manager benchmark is the combination of the individual managers' benchmarks weighted by the plan sponsor's policy allocations to the managers. In this example, the aggregate manager benchmark has less misfit than any of the three managers' individual benchmarks, although the aggregate retains a growth bias relative to the target because of the growth biases of all three managers.

Approaching the issue more generally, Equation 1.4 can be extended to cover the multiple-manager situation. Consider an *aggregate* (denoted by the superscript asterisk) weighted portfolio composed of *m* managers' portfolios; the weights, w_i, are the managers' assigned policy allocations in a sponsor's

Figure 2.2. The Aggregate Manager Benchmark

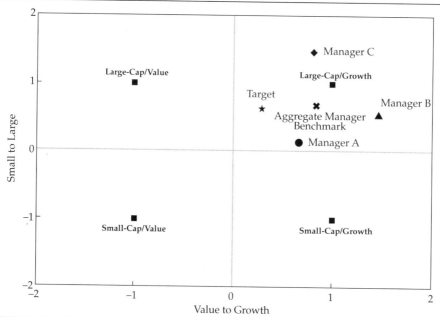

investment program; that is, [1]

$$P_1 = T + (B_1 - T) + A_1 \qquad w_1$$
$$P_2 = T + (B_2 - T) + A_2 \qquad w_2$$
$$P_3 = T + (B_3 - T) + A_3 \qquad w_3$$
$$\cdot \qquad\qquad \cdot$$
$$\cdot \qquad\qquad \cdot$$
$$\cdot \qquad\qquad \cdot$$
$$P_m = T + (B_m - T) + A_m \qquad w_m$$
$$\overline{P^\star = T + (B^\star - T) + A^\star} \qquad \overline{w_{mgrs}{}^\star} \qquad (2.3)$$

In the same way that each manager's portfolio can be segmented into systematic, misfit, and active-management components, so too can the aggregate of the managers' portfolios. The plan sponsor prefers that the performance of the managers, in aggregate, reflect only the performance of the target and the managers' combined active-management returns; that is,

$$P^\star = T + A^\star.$$

The plan sponsor's problem is that $B^\star - T \neq 0$; even in aggregate, the managers still display misfit relative to the target.

Expressing misfit in an aggregate context helps to focus attention on the true nature of the problem. One popular means of conceptualizing the misfit that managers in aggregate bring to an investment program is a Venn diagram. Figure 2.3 presents such an illustration for our simple three-manager example. The background of the diagram represents the composition of the target. The benchmarks of the three managers are superimposed on the target, indicating the managers' respective areas of expertise. The managers overlap in some parts of the target but fail to cover other portions. Misfit risk arises from the possibility that the uncovered areas (both literally and figuratively) will perform differently from the target.

Solution 4: Transport Alpha for the Aggregate Portfolio

The fourth solution to the misfit problem follows directly from applying Equation 2.2 to the entire investment program: Swap the aggregate manager benchmark's return for the target's return. This solution avoids the redundant expenses of the third solution while eliminating misfit before transaction costs.

---

[1]The managers' weights, w_{mgrs}, need not necessarily sum to 100 percent. The plan sponsor may allocate assets to a portfolio specifically designed to control misfit risk (see Misfit Solution 9). For the moment, we can think of w_{mgrs} as the weight of all managers excluding this specialized portfolio's allocation.

Figure 2.3. A Venn Diagram View of Misfit

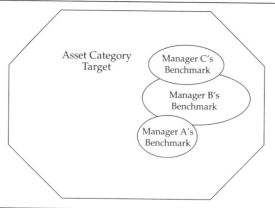

Although this alternative is less expensive than Misfit Solution 3, the transaction has no "natural other side." No investor or market maker stands ready to accept the aggregate manager benchmark's return in exchange for providing the target's return. As a result, a plan sponsor would have to turn to a brokerage firm to implement the swap—undoubtedly an expensive proposition (we have heard anecdotal estimates of 2–3 percent a year)—and the cost would depend on the nature and magnitude of the misfit.[2] Furthermore, the sponsor would have to be aware of counterparty risk associated with the transaction.

Solution 5: Reallocate Funds among Existing Managers

If the current allocations to the managers produce an aggregate manager benchmark with misfit, then perhaps some other set of manager allocations will relieve the problem. Such a solution would be desirable for several reasons. First, the process is relatively easy to explain to the plan's trustees, who may only vaguely grasp the nature of the misfit problem. In fact, because this solution does not involve hiring or firing managers, a plan sponsor's staff might be able to undertake such a reallocation without engaging in a major policy review with the trustees.

A reallocation of funds among the existing managers can be a useful first step because it focuses attention directly on the nature of the misfit problem. In most cases, however, reallocation is unlikely to reduce misfit significantly, particularly without requiring unacceptably large allocations to certain managers. This situation is illustrated in Figure 2.4.

---

[2] In Chapter 1, we estimated that the "cost" of misfit is roughly 14 bps a year. If the cost of solving misfit through a swap is at least 200 bps annually, then this solution is certainly an uneconomical alternative.

Figure 2.4. **Reallocating among Existing Managers**

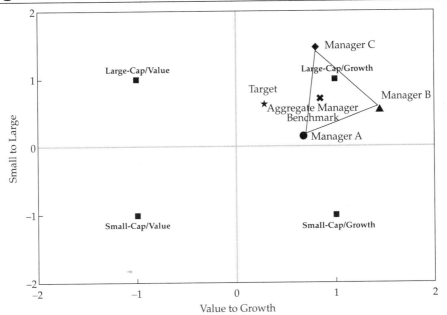

Analyzing portfolios in style space has the convenient attribute that the style coordinates combine linearly in the same way that security betas combine. Thus, a 50/50 combination of manager benchmarks A and B in Figure 2.4 will lie halfway along a straight line connecting the two benchmarks. This feature makes it simple to examine the set of reallocation alternatives open to a plan sponsor.

In our example, the plan sponsor can produce an aggregate manager benchmark with style exposures lying anywhere in the triangle formed at the corners by the three managers' benchmarks.[3] In this example, *no* positive-weight combination of the managers will cause the aggregate manager benchmark to lie on top of (that is, have the same style exposures as) the target.

In some situations, a plan sponsor may be able to eliminate misfit through a reallocation among existing managers, but only at the cost of giving uncomfortably large allocations to one or more managers and significantly reducing allocations to other managers. That is, a particular manager's investment style may effectively complement the investment styles of the other managers. (For

---

[3]This analysis assumes that the policy allocations to the managers are limited to non-negative values. Allowing for negative allocations (i.e., "shorting" a manager or managers) would theoretically permit a sponsor to reach any desired point on the style map.

example, a large-cap/value manager may offset the styles of several small-cap/growth managers.) Achieving the desired style combination, however, may require so large an allocation to the one manager that the sponsor becomes concerned that an active-management error on the part of that manager might unacceptably diminish the total portfolio's performance. In other words, manager reallocation to control misfit may compromise the goal of maintaining adequate diversification of judgment.

The other serious problem with the reallocation solution is that misfit control becomes the dominant factor in manager allocation decisions instead of those allocations being based on expectations concerning managers' value-added capabilities. The managers with the largest allocations may be those providing relatively low expected added value. A plan sponsor may find that the resulting diminution of the total portfolio's expected active-management return is too high a price to pay to eliminate misfit.

Solution 6: Hire an Additional Active Manager

If allocations to the existing managers cannot be altered to produce an acceptable level of misfit, perhaps an additional active manager could be hired to offset the current style biases. Such an alternative is attractive because it provides more flexibility to control misfit and, if properly implemented, it has the potential to virtually eliminate misfit. Furthermore, like the reallocation solution, this alternative is simple to explain to trustees, who need only approve the addition of one more "horse" to the multiple-manager stable.

Figure 2.5 illustrates how this solution would work. Manager D has the value exposure that the plan sponsor's other managers lack. Creating a box connecting all four managers indicates that there is a feasible allocation to the managers that will produce an aggregate manager benchmark with the desired style characteristics.

Despite its appealing simplicity, the additional-manager approach has several serious drawbacks. First, the allocation to the additional manager may have to be quite large to offset the misfit created by the other managers, thereby allowing Manager D to have too much influence over the investment program's performance. In our example, roughly 60 percent of the investment program would have to be allocated to Manager D to offset the growth biases of the other three managers. This lack of diversification of judgment could be controlled by hiring even more managers, but this solution would add significantly to the time expended in manager searches and to management fees paid.

Second, a skillful active manager who coincidentally helps the plan sponsor control misfit may be difficult to find. That such a manager would provide

Figure 2.5. Hiring an Additional Manager

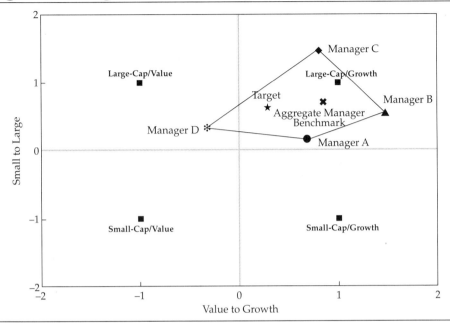

the right style exposures to offset the misfit created by a plan sponsor's other managers would seem fortuitous indeed. To expect that this manager would also be a value-added contributor to the total investment program seems even less realistic. As a result, to achieve acceptable misfit reduction, the sponsor may be forced to hire a manager who provides little or nothing in terms of active-management skills. The misfit horse has been put before the value-added cart.

Third, and perhaps most importantly, the misfit problem is dynamic, potentially changing from period to period. What happens if the plan sponsor chooses to alter the manager alignment, perhaps firing an existing manager and replacing that manager with another or simply deciding to allocate more funds to an existing manager and less to another? The manager hired to control misfit may no longer solve the puzzle because the aggregate manager benchmark will have changed along with the manager alignment. Should the misfit-control manager now be fired and another hired? Although possible, such a process would seem irresponsibly expensive, both in transaction costs and manager search efforts.

Solution 7: Use an Index Fund

By definition, if a plan sponsor retains no active managers and instead places all of its assets in a passively managed portfolio designed to track the target, then the investment program will have no misfit. Extending this logic, we might conclude that investing a portion of heretofore actively managed assets in an index fund is a viable misfit-control option.

Although such an approach will certainly reduce misfit, it does so inefficiently and at a high price. Viewed in style space, the index fund lies on top of the target. Consequently, it cannot be as effective at offsetting misfit as the additional-manager solution (or other solutions, as we will see shortly). If a boat is listing to one side, shifting a certain amount of weight to the center of the boat will relieve some of the tilt but not as efficiently as shifting the same weight to the other side of the boat. Furthermore, because an index fund has a zero (actually, slightly negative) expected active-management return, taking assets from the active managers and placing them in an index fund will reduce the investment program's expected value-added returns.

If the plan sponsor has not previously used passive management, it makes little sense to sacrifice positive expected value of active management to control misfit through the use of an index fund. Other solutions will do a better job at a lower expected value-added cost. If the sponsor already has an index fund in place, then the plan can actually increase its expected value-added returns and/or reduce its misfit by replacing the index fund with a customized misfit-control portfolio.

Solution 8: Combine Style Portfolios

As institutional investors have come to understand the impact of managers' investment styles on performance, various organizations have developed domestic equity investment style indexes. In several instances, enterprising managers have created passively managed portfolios designed to track the performance of these generic style indexes. A plan sponsor can now mix and match investment style portfolios to create a wide range of style combinations at relatively low management fees. As a result, one possible means of controlling misfit is to create a combination of style portfolios that specifically offsets any misfit present in the investment program.

Figure 2.6 shows how style portfolios might be applied to the misfit problem. Given the aggregate manager benchmark of the plan sponsor's three managers, a combination of the four style portfolios is produced such that the joint allocations to the three managers and the style combination creates investment style exposures precisely equal to those of the target.

The style-combination solution has several important advantages over the previously discussed alternatives. It focuses solely on the misfit problem. The plan sponsor, knowing that the style-combination portfolio will be able to

Figure 2.6. Combining Style Portfolios

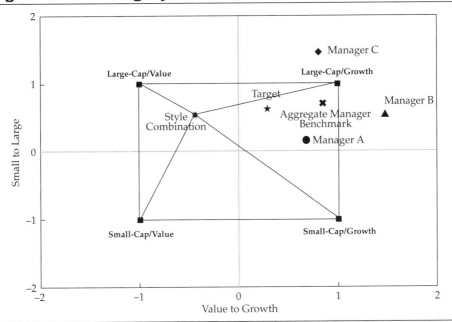

correct for any subsequent misfit, is free to concentrate on hiring the most proficient active managers. Moreover, this solution provides a customized approach to controlling misfit that can be adjusted to accommodate changing circumstances.

The style-combination solution does have several disadvantages. The required style combination may lie "outside the box"; that is, no positive-weight combination of the style portfolios is offsetting the misfit of the plan sponsor's managers. In that case, short selling one or more of the style portfolios may be necessary. Given the relatively concentrated positions most of these portfolios hold, shorting the component securities in large volume may prove difficult.

The style-combination solution also is a complex approach that is not easily explained to trustees. They must understand that a portion of the total portfolio's assets is being devoted to misfit-risk control with no expectation of value-added return. Moreover, the style-combination portfolio is likely to produce returns quite different from those of the active managers. These differences may cause considerable distress among the trustees during periods when the style-combination portfolio underperforms the other managers' actual and benchmark portfolios.

A more subtle, but nevertheless important, disadvantage of the style-combination solution is that it can generate considerable industry- and security-specific risk relative to the target. For example, small-cap/value style indexes usually are heavily concentrated in banks and utilities. Consequently, although the combination of style portfolios may display acceptable common factor risk characteristics, the underlying industry- and stock-specific misfit risk may still be present and compromise the performance of the misfit-control portfolio.

Solution 9: Create a Zero-Misfit Dynamic Completeness Fund

In Equation 2.3, the aggregate portfolio of a plan sponsor's managers was segmented in the following manner:

$$P^* = T + (B^* - T) + A^*.$$

Now, define a hedge portfolio, H (that is, a portfolio of long and short positions that in total has no net dollar investment), with the following attributes:

$$H = T - B^*. \tag{2.4}$$

If we were to combine this hedge portfolio with the plan sponsor's aggregate portfolio, the result would be

$$P^* = T + (B^* - T) + A^*$$
$$+ H = (T - B^*) + 0$$
$$\overline{P^* + H = T + 0 + A^*.} \tag{2.5}$$

Misfit has been eliminated and the joint portfolio has become the target plus the managers' added value, which is the plan sponsor's desired solution. We call this hedge portfolio a zero-misfit *dynamic completeness fund* (DCF). Figure 2.7 illustrates the application of a *zero-misfit DCF*.

In many ways, the zero-misfit DCF solution is similar to the combined style portfolio approach. In both cases, a customized portfolio is created that is directed solely toward misfit control. Like the combined-style portfolio, the zero-misfit DCF can accommodate changes in the sponsor's manager alignment. The zero-misfit DCF has a significant advantage over the combined-style portfolio, however, in that, by definition, it has no industry- or stock-specific risk relative to the target. The zero-misfit DCF is constructed to offset precisely the stock-by-stock over- or underexposures of the aggregate manager benchmark relative to the target.[4] For example, in Table 1.3, if the

---

[4] Significantly, the zero-misfit DCF is a true nonparametric solution to the misfit problem. No risk model is required to construct the zero-misfit DCF.

Figure 2.7. The Zero-Misfit DCF Solution

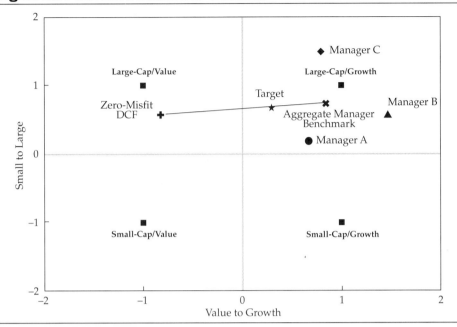

benchmark were the aggregate manager benchmark of the plan sponsor's active managers and Security 1 had a weighting of 21 percent in the benchmark and 13 percent in the target, then the zero-misfit DCF would have a holding of –8 percent in Security 1.

Because it addresses the misfit problem on an individual-security basis, the zero-misfit DCF approach is the most effective method of eliminating misfit. Furthermore, because the zero-misfit DCF is a hedge portfolio, it requires no cash outlay on the part of the plan sponsor.[5] All of the sponsor's assets can be directed to the most productive active managers, thereby allowing the plan sponsor to maximize the investment program's information ratio.

The zero-misfit DCF has serious drawbacks, however. As a hedge portfolio, the zero-misfit DCF carries short positions in those securities that are overweighted in the aggregate manager benchmark relative to the target. In practice, implementing these short sales may prove difficult. Furthermore, like the style-combination approach, the zero-misfit DCF suffers from more complexity than the less sophisticated approaches. Moreover, the zero-misfit

[5]The zero-misfit DCF does not necessarily have a zero net asset value. For purposes of introducing the DCF concept, we mention only the hedge portfolio version of the zero-misfit DCF. In some situations, the zero-misfit DCF will have a positive net asset value.

DCF portfolio, like the style-combination portfolio, may produce returns quite different from any generated by the plan's other managers, potentially causing concern among the plan's trustees.

Solution 10: Create a Constrained DCF

If plan sponsors were free to sell short securities with no administrative complications and no significant additional expenses, then the zero-misfit DCF would be the most effective solution to the misfit problem. With the advent of market-neutral investment strategies, the mechanisms for creating low-cost long/short portfolios have advanced considerably in recent years.[6] Nevertheless, most plan sponsors are reluctant to commit significant assets to such portfolios, particularly if those portfolios involve many short positions in small, illiquid names. For that reason, sponsors find investing in a zero-misfit DCF impractical. Instead, they prefer a DCF portfolio that either holds only long positions or constrains the number and size of any short positions. In either case, this constrained portfolio is no longer a hedge portfolio. Rather, it has a positive net asset value. We refer to this DCF as a *constrained DCF*.

The construction of a constrained DCF is similar to the process involved in managing an index fund: Produce returns that track those of a specified benchmark. In this case, the zero-misfit DCF serves as the index whose returns are to be replicated. The constrained DCF is created using standard index fund management procedures, such as optimization techniques and stratified sampling methods.

Figure 2.8 provides a view of the constrained DCF relative to the zero-misfit DCF. In general, because of its limits on short positions, the constrained DCF yields less-extreme style exposures than does the zero-misfit DCF. Depending on the composition of the misfit portfolio, this constraint may or may not be seriously binding in terms of the constrained DCF's ability to mimic the zero-misfit DCF's performance.

The constrained DCF has the misfit-control focus and flexibility of both the style-combination and zero-misfit DCF solutions. It offers much of the stock-specific misfit control lacking in the style-combination solution. At the same time, it avoids the problems of shorting stocks associated with the zero-misfit DCF solution. The optimization techniques typically used to build the constrained DCF can also be used to limit turnover and trading costs.

On the downside, the shorting constraint may hinder the constrained DCF's ability to compensate for the misfit generated by the aggregate manager benchmark. Instead of complete stock-by-stock misfit control, as provided by

---

[6]The mechanics of long/short investing are described in Jacobs and Levy (1993).

Figure 2.8. The Constrained DCF Solution

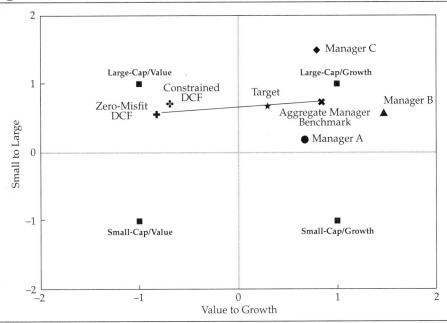

the zero-misfit DCF, the constrained DCF relies more on sector weightings and factor exposures to reduce misfit. The more extreme the style exposures of the misfit portfolio, the more difficult the task of offsetting those exposures with a long-only or limited-short-position portfolio.

In addition, constrained DCF, like the style-combination solution, has the disadvantage that assets must be diverted from the active managers, thereby reducing the expected value-added return of the investment program. Moreover, like the style-combination and zero-misfit DCF solutions, the constrained DCF can be difficult to describe to plan trustees.

3. Managing a Dynamic Completeness Fund

Creating and maintaining a dynamic completeness fund requires coordinating and implementing a set of diverse assignments. Typically, three separate organizations share responsibility for DCF management: the plan sponsor, a DCF "builder," and a DCF manager. Although one organization could conceivably carry out more than one part of the entire process, the technical skills needed to implement a DCF are sufficiently varied and complex to invite a division of labor.

The Plan Sponsor

As the owner of funds, the plan sponsor retains ultimate authority and responsibility for misfit control. In the campaign to control misfit, the sponsor assumes the role of general—setting broad strategy and directing the troops. Only the sponsor should make decisions that have investment policy implications because only the sponsor bears the ultimate financial consequences of those decisions. Yet, rarely does the sponsor have the expertise necessary to specify the DCF's composition or actually manage the DCF portfolio. Sponsors contribute the most value to the misfit-control process when they

- define the target;
- establish the policy allocations for non-DCF and DCF managers;
- coordinate development, collection, and evaluation of manager benchmarks;
- evaluate performance of both the active and the DCF managers and evaluate the DCF builder's effectiveness.

Defining the Target. The target is the cornerstone of the DCF construction process. It expresses the essence of the plan sponsor's investment program within an asset category. No one "correct" target exists for any asset category. The primary requirements are that the target be consistent with the sponsor's risk tolerance from the perspective of expected risk and return, be preferred to alternative targets, and be investable. The sponsor's beliefs about how the capital markets reward various sources of risk in the long run determine the appropriate target.

The target resembles a manager's benchmark, in that it is composed of an identifiable set of securities and associated weights. The plan sponsor must make arrangements to deliver the target's composition to the DCF builder in advance of the DCF's construction. If the target is a standard market index, this step is unlikely to prove troublesome, because the index's constituents and associated weights are readily available. If the target has customized elements, however, then the sponsor must fit construction and delivery of the target into the DCF production schedule.

Establishing Policy Allocations. Policy allocations to non-DCF and DCF managers reflect the plan sponsor's expectations regarding the relative rewards and risks the managers bring to the investment program. The sponsor could ignore the misfit problem, as in Misfit Solution 1. The assets would then be naively divided equally among the non-DCF managers and the allocations allowed to drift over time, depending on the managers' relative returns. Of course, making no decision is tantamount to making a decision. The managers will end up with some set of allocations, even if achieved by default. Those allocations will affect both the misfit and the active-management returns the investment program experiences. Preferably, then, the sponsor will take a proactive approach and determine its manager allocations in a systematic process known as *manager structuring.*[1]

The objective of manager structuring is to assign manager allocations so that the aggregate manager portfolio offers the most attractive combination of expected return and volatility of returns relative to the target. Manager structuring requires the plan sponsor to make assumptions about the managers' expected misfit and value-added returns, the variability of those returns, and the extent to which the returns tend to move together. These expectations can be developed in a number of ways, but typically, the sponsor uses the past as a window to the future. The sponsor first collects historical data on the average levels and variances of the managers' misfit and active-management returns and then calculates the covariances of those returns among the managers.

After examining the historical information, the plan sponsor then makes adjustments as it deems appropriate to create expected values for the variables. Although rules-based approaches can be used, these modifications often require subjective decisions.[2] Should a particular manager's historical value-added returns be scaled back? Is the misfit covariance for a certain pair

---

[1]Why plan sponsors use multiple-manager investment structures is an interesting topic that has not received much attention. Three articles on the subject are Sharpe (1981), Barry and Starks (1984), and Jeffrey (1991).

[2]For example, the plan sponsor might believe that the historical value added by a particular manager was exceptionally high and is unlikely to recur in the future. In that case, the sponsor might reduce the expected value-added goal to a more reasonable level. Ambachtsheer (1977) offers a quantitative procedure for adjusting manager historical "alphas."

of managers likely to be higher than what was actually observed in the past? In the end, the decision to deploy active management is a large leap of faith in itself, so the sponsor should not shy away from making additional "educated guesses" concerning the expected risk–return attributes of its managers. Manager structuring simply provides a disciplined framework for making those decisions.

At this point, the plan sponsor has a set of expected returns and a variance–covariance matrix for the misfit and active-management processes of its managers. Applying the benchmark orthogonality properties, the sponsor can compute the expected return and variability of returns relative to the target for any set of allocations to the managers. A quadratic optimization procedure creates an efficient frontier of the risk and return combinations formed by alternative sets of manager allocations. Various constraints (for example, maximum or minimum manager allocations) can be placed on the optimization to add more realism to the analysis. As the final step, given the plan sponsor's risk tolerance, its decision makers must select a point on the efficient frontier that represents a desired combination of aggregate expected added value relative to the target and expected variability of returns relative to the target.[3]

Manager structuring can be used to generate efficient combinations of existing managers corresponding to Misfit Solution 5. Alternatively, the plan sponsor might include expected misfit and active-management returns and risks for an additional non-DCF manager (or managers), thereby producing efficient allocations to existing and new managers akin to Misfit Solution 6. The manager-structuring process can be applied using a zero-misfit or constrained DCF portfolio as one of the candidate managers, as described in Misfit Solutions 9 and 10.

Coordinating Manager Benchmarks. Effective misfit control requires the availability of valid benchmarks for the investment program's current and prospective managers. The plan sponsor must ensure that such benchmarks are created, maintained, and periodically delivered to the DCF builder to permit construction of the aggregate manager benchmark. Ideally, all managers will assume responsibility for supplying the DCF builder with valid benchmarks on a timely basis. More likely, however, the sponsor will have to prod certain managers to develop and deliver their benchmarks. In the extreme, the sponsor may have to produce its own benchmarks for recalcitrant managers.

Regardless of the source of the benchmarks, the plan sponsor should

---

[3]Our research indicates that plan sponsors are much more risk averse with their active-management allocations than with their asset category allocations, by a factor of roughly 10:1.

periodically confirm their validity. Inappropriate benchmarks will misrepresent the managers' investment styles, leading to misguided misfit-control efforts. Tests of benchmark quality examine the ability of a benchmark to capture a manager's investment style.[4] We recommend the use of eight specific evaluation criteria:

- *High coverage.* The proportion of the manager's actual portfolio contained in the benchmark is large.
- *Low turnover.* The proportion of the benchmark's market value allocated to purchases and sales during periodic rebalancings is manageable from a trading cost perspective.
- *Positive active positions.* Those securities whose weights in the manager's actual portfolio exceed their corresponding weights in the benchmark constitute a large proportion of the manager's actual portfolio.
- *Investable position sizes.* Securities are represented in proportions in the benchmark that could realistically be owned by the manager if all the manager's assets were invested in the benchmark.
- *Reduced observed active-management risk.* Given the manager's past returns, the active-management risk calculated using the specific benchmark under review is less than the active-management risk calculated using a broad market index as the benchmark.
- *Significantly positive extramarket correlation between actual portfolio returns and benchmark returns.* The correlation of historical extramarket returns for the manager's actual portfolio versus the extramarket returns on the benchmark is statistically greater than zero.
- *Insignificant extramarket correlation between value-added returns and benchmark returns.* The correlation of historical extramarket value-added returns versus the extramarket returns on the benchmark is statistically indistinguishable from zero.
- *Similar style exposures between the actual portfolio and the benchmark.* Over time, plots of the benchmark and the actual portfolio in style space cluster in close proximity.

The plan sponsor should insist that the manager provide a proof statement attesting to his or her benchmark's quality before formally approving the benchmark for the first time. Thereafter, the plan sponsor should conduct quality tests on a regular basis to ensure that the benchmark continues to function at an adequate level. The failure of a benchmark to pass these quality tests indicates fundamental problems with its construction and points to the need for corrective measures. The sponsor should accept without further

---

[4] For a discussion of benchmark quality tests, see Bailey (1992).

question a benchmark passing the quality tests. If the sponsor promotes the manager's ownership of the benchmark, then it should not micromanage the benchmark's design.

Evaluating Manager and DCF Builder Performance. A plan sponsor should adopt a formal manager-continuation policy as part of its overall investment policy. A manager-continuation policy explicitly states both the quantitative and qualitative criteria the sponsor uses to evaluate its managers. On the quantitative side, the sponsor works with its managers to establish mutually acceptable performance targets, specified in terms of expected value-added returns and the variability of those value-added returns (effectively, the information ratio). Periodically, the sponsor should compare actual performance with expected performance and make judgments concerning the managers' value-added capabilities.

Drawing conclusions about manager skill from historical performance data is difficult, however, because of the large normal variation in managers' investment results. Sponsors thus invariably supplement quantitative performance data with qualitative observations about the stability of managers' organizations, retention of key personnel, the consistency with which the investment processes are applied, and so on.

Applied in a disciplined fashion, manager-continuation policies help sponsors avoid hasty reactions to recent poor performance, thus preventing excessive manager turnover. Although plan sponsors cannot (and will not) ignore past performance in conducting their manager evaluations, such quantitative information should carry less weight than the qualitative insights about the manager's organization and investment process. A sponsor witnessing negative value-added results should ask "What has fundamentally changed in the manager's operation?" If the answer is "nothing," then given the high probability that even the most skillful managers will experience occasional—and possibly extended—periods of disappointing results, the sponsor should be patient.

Although the DCF builder does not directly manage assets, the plan sponsor should also evaluate the builder's performance as part of its manager-continuation policy. Just as investment managers have quantitative performance targets specified in advance, so too should performance expectations be developed for the DCF builder. Similar to its evaluation of managers, the sponsor should apply qualitative criteria to evaluating the DCF builder.

The DCF Builder

The DCF builder plays an intermediary role in the DCF's production. The DCF builder acts as a consultant to the plan sponsor in both the design of the

DCF and the structuring of managers within the total portfolio. The DCF builder also works with the DCF manager to produce the DCF manager's benchmark and to facilitate low-cost implementation of the DCF portfolio. The DCF builder has the following tasks:

- assist the plan sponsor in developing an efficient manager structure;
- build and rebalance the zero-misfit DCF;
- build, rebalance, and deliver the constrained DCF to the DCF manager; and
- monitor DCF performance and report to the plan sponsor.

Assisting in the Manager-Structuring Process. Although the plan sponsor bears ultimate responsibility for selecting allocations to the non-DCF and DCF managers, the DCF builder has access to information and tools that can facilitate the structuring process. As an integral part of its business, the DCF builder acts as a repository for manager benchmark data, including historical asset lists and rates of return. Those same archiving capabilities can be used to collect historical data on the composition of the managers' actual portfolios and returns. The index-matching algorithms the DCF builder uses to construct a constrained DCF can be applied to computing efficient combinations of existing and prospective managers.

The manager-structuring process is typically an iterative procedure. The DCF builder uses its accumulated knowledge of manager risk–return profiles to help the plan sponsor develop a consistent set of manager misfit and value-added return expectations. Often, the original assumptions produce unrealistic manager allocations, causing the sponsor to reconsider those assumptions. The process of making modifications usually offers valuable insights into the managers' value-added capabilities. In fact, our experience has been that setting up the structuring analysis is just as valuable to the sponsor as the final conclusions.

Building and Rebalancing the Zero-Misfit DCF. The zero-misfit DCF is the portfolio that, on a stock-by-stock basis, precisely offsets the misfit of the aggregate manager benchmark relative to the target. The zero-misfit DCF has the property that when combined with the aggregate manager benchmark, it produces a portfolio equivalent to the target. Although its definition is simple, the steps involved in producing the zero-misfit DCF are far from trivial.

The DCF builder constructs the zero-misfit DCF at regular intervals. To do so, it first creates the aggregate manager benchmark based on the managers' benchmarks and the sponsor's manager allocations. Each stock in each manager's benchmark is multiplied by the manager's allocation. Summing across all stocks in all of the managers' benchmarks gives the composition of the aggregate manager benchmark. The DCF builder then computes the zero-misfit DCF by taking the weight of each stock in the target and subtracting the stock's corresponding weight in the aggregate manager benchmark. (Note that the misfit portfolio's holdings equal those of the zero-misfit DCF in absolute value but are of the opposite sign.)

The managers' benchmark-rebalancing schedules dictate the frequency of the DCF's rebalancing. Usually, manager benchmarks are rebalanced on a quarterly or semiannual basis. Changes in the managers' benchmarks result in a corresponding change in the aggregate manager benchmark, which in turn generates shifts in the zero-misfit DCF. Rebalancing the DCF less frequently than the manager benchmarks would cause the zero-misfit DCF to become misaligned with the aggregate manager benchmark, thus diminishing the DCF's misfit-control capability.

Even if the managers' benchmarks have not changed in membership over a particular time period, changes in the composition of the target may require rebalancing of the zero-misfit DCF. For example, takeovers and mergers regularly alter the makeup of market indexes. In those situations, particularly if the changes involve large-cap stocks, substantial misfit can be created that must be offset by adjustments to the zero-misfit DCF.

Changes in the plan sponsor's manager roster also require modifications in the zero-misfit DCF. Those manager changes may arise from the sponsor's decision to dismiss a manager or add a new one or simply to reallocate funds among existing managers. In any case, the aggregate manager benchmark will be affected, thus altering the zero-misfit DCF.

Building, Rebalancing, and Delivering the Constrained DCF to the DCF Manager. Ideally, the plan sponsor would be able to use the zero-misfit DCF as its misfit-control instrument. Because of practical limitations on the short positions the DCF holds, however, the sponsor will almost certainly substitute a constrained DCF. Therefore, the DCF builder's assignment is to design a constrained DCF that not only satisfies the sponsor's designated short-selling restrictions but also adequately tracks the returns of the zero-misfit DCF.

Generally, managers use two approaches to construct index-replicating portfolios: stratified sampling and optimization. Stratified sampling involves two steps: First, the manager matches the weights of the targeted index's largest holdings. Second, the manager purchases other securities in the index so that key characteristics of the portfolio, such as industry weights, equal those of the index. Optimization uses a risk model and a quadratic optimization procedure to examine combinations of securities, identifying that combination expected to replicate the index's returns with the least variability over time.

Most U.S. domestic equity index fund managers use stratified sampling methods to mimic the performance of broad, cap-weighted indexes. Our experience has been, however, that optimization works better in tracking non-cap-weighted portfolios that exhibit nonmarketlike style exposures. The aggregate manager benchmark and the zero-misfit DCF are usually not cap weighted. Furthermore, the financial characteristics (e.g., price/earnings, price/book, and financial leverage) are important in defining the style exposures of the zero-misfit DCF. Standard stratified sampling methods are not readily capable of dealing with the diverse nature of these style exposures. Because optimization is usually based on a risk model that accounts explicitly for these exposures, it can better define a portfolio that has style characteristics matching those of the zero-misfit DCF.

The DCF builder must deliver the constrained DCF to the DCF manager prior to the start of the evaluation period. The DCF builder should give the DCF manager adequate time to examine the DCF and request modifications. The DCF builder is limited by the requirement that it produce an investable benchmark for the DCF manager. In particular, the DCF builder must be cognizant of the need to control turnover in the constrained DCF during rebalancings and ensure that adequate liquidity exists for the position sizes assigned to securities in the constrained DCF. For example, the DCF builder may determine that a large position in XYZ security significantly improves the tracking ability of the constrained DCF this quarter. Nevertheless, if that large position contributes to excessive turnover from the previous quarter's portfolio or if the DCF manager can acquire that security only at an unreasonable transaction cost, the security will have to be excluded or its position size reduced.

The zero-misfit DCF rebalancing schedule determines when rebalancings of the constrained DCF should occur. Even if the component securities in the manager benchmarks and the target remain constant, periodic rebalancings of the constrained DCF will still be required to avoid "style" drift: Over time, the weights of securities in the constrained DCF will move as a result of market action. In addition, the securities' financial attributes may change. The result is a shift in the constrained DCF's style exposures that the DCF builder must account for if misfit is to remain under control. Longer than semiannual rebalancings run the risk of tardy responses to this style drift.

Monitoring and Reporting DCF Performance. The benchmark for the DCF builder is the zero-misfit DCF. That is, the DCF builder is charged with creating a constrained portfolio that tracks the zero-misfit DCF's performance within tolerances agreed on in advance with the plan sponsor. The effectiveness of that process is measured by comparing the performance of the constrained DCF with that of the zero-misfit DCF.

The zero-misfit DCF, by definition, eliminates all misfit *ex ante*. Because of its limitations on short sales, however, and the investability requirement, the constrained DCF cannot be expected to remove misfit entirely. The degree of misfit risk reduction depends on the short-selling constraints imposed on the DCF builder and on the magnitude of the existing misfit. The greater the limits on short selling and the more extreme the style exposures of the aggregate manager benchmark, the greater the tracking error of the constrained DCF relative to the zero-misfit DCF and the lower the reduction in misfit risk. Our experience has been that more than 50 percent of misfit risk can typically be eliminated by the constrained DCF.

Because of its intermediary role in the DCF construction process, the DCF builder is well positioned to report on the effectiveness of the misfit-control program. Because it creates both the zero-misfit and constrained DCFs, it has ready access to the returns on those two portfolios and, therefore, can analyze the effectiveness of its own contribution to misfit-risk control. Moreover, because of its frequent contact with the DCF manager, the DCF builder can also collect performance data on the actual DCF portfolio and report on the efficacy of the DCF manager's efforts to control misfit risk.

The DCF builder should regularly produce a DCF performance analysis for the plan sponsor. At a minimum, that report should include

- recent returns on the aggregate manager benchmark, the zero-misfit DCF, the constrained DCF, and the DCF manager's portfolio;
- the relative performance of various alternative approaches to misfit-risk control;
- attribution analysis identifying sources of deviation between the zero-misfit DCF's returns and those of the constrained DCF and between the constrained DCF and the DCF portfolio created by the DCF manager; and
- updated numbers on the historical misfit experience, both cumulative and since the inception of the DCF.

The DCF performance report serves both educational and fiduciary purposes. It increases the plan sponsor decision makers' understanding and awareness about the misfit problem. It also offers a means for the plan sponsor to monitor the effectiveness of the misfit-control operation.

The DCF Manager

The DCF manager, on the front lines of the misfit-control effort, has responsibility for creating and maintaining a portfolio of securities (the *invested DCF*) that adequately tracks the performance of the constrained DCF. To fulfill this role, the DCF manager

- evaluates the investability of the constrained DCF received from the DCF builder;
- manages the trade-off between transaction costs and tracking error; and
- creates an invested DCF portfolio that matches or exceeds the performance of the constrained DCF benchmark within predetermined tracking-error tolerances.

Evaluating the Investability of the Constrained DCF. The DCF manager's role resembles that of a standard index fund manager. That is, like an index fund manager, the DCF manager is assigned a specific benchmark and charged with constructing an actual portfolio that replicates the returns on that benchmark. The DCF manager's job is more difficult, however, than that of a typical passive manager. Most importantly, the benchmark assigned to the DCF manager is not a broad market index, such as the S&P 500. Instead, the benchmark is the constrained DCF. Each DCF assignment is different from all others because each plan sponsor presents a unique set of manager benchmarks and allocations. The constrained DCF is a customized set of securities, with potentially significant nonmarket style exposures and a composition that changes over time.

The unique nature of the constrained DCF requires the DCF manager to possess a sophisticated set of portfolio-management tools. The DCF manager must be able to analyze any security appearing in the constrained DCF. At a minimum, the DCF manager must have access to a large database of securities and a multifactor risk model. As a result, traditional managers, who select portfolios based on fundamental analysis of a relatively small set of securities, generally have difficulty carrying out the DCF manager assignment. Potential DCF managers usually are restricted to the set of organizations that use model-driven valuation approaches and specialize in accepting customized assignments.

The DCF manager receives the constrained DCF prior to the start of an evaluation period. The DCF manager loads the security holdings into its own portfolio analytics system and evaluates the constrained DCF's investment characteristics. Charged with the responsibility for tracking its performance, the DCF manager must carefully evaluate the investability of the constrained DCF. Is turnover from the previous period manageable? Are position sizes of certain securities too large to acquire at acceptable transaction costs? Any concerns must be promptly referred back to the DCF builder for resolution.

Controlling Transaction Costs. Once the constrained DCF has been finalized, the DCF manager prepares a trading program to move from the existing invested DCF portfolio to a new portfolio. Ideally, he or she will own all securities in the constrained DCF at their prescribed weights. Index fund managers refer to this procedure as "full replication."

In a world without transaction costs, full replication would ensure that the invested DCF precisely matched the performance of the constrained DCF. Trading securities is not a costless activity, however. Therefore, the DCF manager must evaluate the performance-tracking effects of including each of the constrained DCF's securities in the invested DCF. Before transaction costs, more securities unambiguously increase tracking ability. After transaction costs, the marginal benefit of including a particular security may be negative.

Similar to the DCF builder preparing the constrained DCF, the DCF manager will use either a stratified sampling or an optimization approach to construct the invested DCF. Again, our experience has been that optimization is the more effective method, in that it can explicitly account for the style exposures of the constrained DCF. It also has the advantage that the impact of transaction costs on performance tracking can be built directly into the design of the portfolio.

As is the case with any index fund manager, the DCF manager needs access to low-cost trading facilities, including internal and external crossing systems. Many, or all, of the trades the DCF manager executes will be informationless, in the sense that they convey no knowledge of relative valuations. Rather, they will be conducted merely to track the constrained DCF's performance. The DCF manager wants to avoid paying a premium simply to adjust the portfolio. Passive trading skills are essential to effective DCF portfolio management.

Matching or Exceeding Benchmark Performance. The DCF manager may take a passive approach to investing the DCF portfolio, in which case the invested DCF is designed to match the performance of the constrained DCF less transaction costs and management fees. Alternatively, the DCF manager may take an active approach, in which case the invested DCF is expected to exceed the performance of the constrained DCF benchmark net of fees and expenses. Typically, active management is carried out under strict risk-control policies designed to prevent unacceptably volatile returns relative to the benchmark. (The terms "semipassive management" or "enhanced indexing" are often applied to this approach.)

The primary advantage of the passive approach is that it retains the focus on the DCF's reason for existence: to control misfit risk. The DCF manager's ability to track the returns on the constrained DCF stands out clearly for performance evaluation purposes. Conceptually, there is no reason why the passive approach should not be effective if the plan sponsor understands that the dynamic nature of the DCF will result in increased transaction costs and more volatile tracking performance than a standard S&P 500 index fund manager would incur.

Our experience has been, however, that index fund managers have a difficult time with the DCF assignment. We suspect that the problems are related to the noncapitalization weighting of the DCF's constituent securities and its dynamic composition, both features not confronted in an ordinary passive-management assignment. As a result, active managers, with tightly disciplined risk-control procedures and with experience handling custom investment mandates, may be more-effective DCF managers than passive managers would be. Also, their active-management skills may permit them to defray some of the extra transaction costs associated with managing a DCF portfolio.

Recapping the DCF Construction Process

The DCF construction process entails a number of steps, usually carried out by three separate organizations that must coordinate their efforts if they are to accomplish the objective of controlling misfit risk. Exhibit 3.1 summarizes the responsibilities and interactions of the parties responsible for successfully implementing a DCF.

Exhibit 3.1. The DCF Construction Process

Inputs	Outputs	Feedback and Control
Select asset category target (plan sponsor)	Define DCF (DCF builder) Zero-misfit DCF benchmark Constrained DCF benchmark	Report on DCF portfolio (DCF manager)
Determine manager allocation (plan sponsor and DCF builder) Identify benchmarks for each manager Establish policy allocation to each benchmark/manager Determine appropriate allocation for DCF portfolio	Create invested DCF portfolio (DCF manager)	Evaluate misfit control (DCF builder)
Create aggregate manager benchmark (DCF builder)		

4. DCF Case Studies

Although recognition of the style bias phenomenon dates back to the late 1970s, only in the past 15 years have plan sponsors begun to actually apply formal misfit-control techniques. Some plan sponsors acknowledge the problem but have chosen not to act; they are willing to accept the cost of misfit. Others have taken positive steps to limit misfit by restructuring the allocations to their existing managers or by hiring additional active managers with misfit-reducing investment styles. Still others have turned to a DCF solution as the most systematic and efficient means of minimizing misfit.

The earliest domestic equity DCFs were initiated in the mid-1980s. During the past decade, a half-dozen large institutional investors put DCFs into place. Thus, only now has sufficient history been accumulated to permit empirical analysis of how DCFs operate in real time.

A Tale of Three Plan Sponsors

This chapter reports the misfit-control experiences of three plan sponsors, all of which were included in the misfit-risk study presented in Chapter 1. These organizations were selected not only because they have had DCFs in place for several years but also because they differ notably in their non-DCF manager alignments. As a result, each organization presents a different misfit problem and DCF solution. We compare and contrast the pre-DCF situation facing each plan sponsor, the characteristics of the DCF that resolved the misfit problem, and the actual misfit experienced once the DCF was implemented.

All three plan sponsors operate multibillion-dollar pension funds. Diamond is a basic materials firm with a $1.1 billion domestic equity investment program. Ivory is a large public fund that invests $13.3 billion in domestic equities. Ruby is a capital goods firm that holds $1.3 billion in domestic equities.

The plan sponsors vary in their approaches to structuring managers:
- Diamond has always used active managers to run its domestic equity program. It was a natural step, then, when the DCF manager initially was hired, to assign that manager an active-management (albeit low-volatility) mandate.

- Ivory has traditionally indexed a large portion of its domestic equities. Although its DCF managers now actively manage the DCF portfolio in a low-volatility style, the invested DCF portfolio was managed passively for some time. Ivory also uses a manager to invest passively in a portfolio indexed to the asset category target. In total, the majority of the plan's assets are invested through the DCF and the target-based index fund.
- Ruby, in the past, indexed roughly one-third of its domestic equity portfolio to a large-capitalization benchmark with slightly different characteristics from those of the target. The other two-thirds were actively managed by several firms that, in aggregate, possessed rather extreme investment style exposures. With the implementation of a DCF, Ruby replaced its passive manager with a low-active-risk DCF manager and maintained its aggressive active-manager style exposures.

The Pre-DCF Situation

Each plan sponsor retained a group of active domestic equity managers whose aggregate manager benchmark varied from the target, thereby generating misfit. The differences among the plan sponsors' multiple-manager investment programs help to explain the differing characteristics of their DCF misfit solutions.

The Risk–Return Experience. Figures 4.1 and 4.2 present information regarding the performance of the three organizations' domestic equity programs prior to their establishment of DCFs. Figure 4.1 illustrates the return side of that performance, and Figure 4.2 shows the variability of those returns.[1] The two figures separate the domestic equity performance results into active management ($P - B$) and misfit ($B - T$) components and then combine those two sources of return to show performance relative to the target ($P - T$), or *excess target return*.

As Figure 4.1 demonstrates, the value-added returns of the three plan sponsors varied widely, although all three organizations' managers were able, on an aggregate basis, to essentially match the performance of their benchmarks (net of fees) and, in the case of Diamond and Ruby, substantially exceed their benchmarks' returns. Misfit returns, on the other hand, were uniformly negative. As a result of these negative misfit returns, the domestic equity programs of Diamond and Ivory underperformed their targets. In the case of Ruby, the active-management returns were strong enough to overcome the

---

[1]The length of time over which performance was measured in the pre-DCF period depended on the availability of data from the plan sponsors. The particular periods covered are listed at the bottom of each sponsor's bar cluster.

Figure 4.1. Pre-DCF Returns

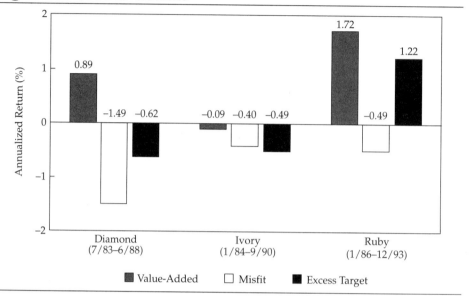

Figure 4.2. Pre-DCF Return Variability

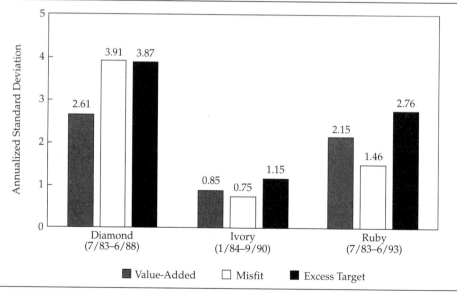

head wind of a sizable negative misfit return and produce a positive excess target return.

There is no reason for these misfit returns to have been negative. The expected risk-adjusted misfit return is zero. Presumably over another period of time, the misfit return for any (or all) of these three plan sponsors could have been positive. It is not a coincidence, however, that the plan sponsors all chose to tackle their misfit problems after experiencing negative misfit returns. Adverse outcomes have a way of focusing decision makers' attention on the root causes of their problems.

Figure 4.2 displays the risk side of the three plan sponsors' pre-DCF domestic equity results. Diamond, because of its all-active-management approach, experienced the highest active-management, misfit, and excess target risk. Ivory, with its considerable passive-management orientation, had relatively low volatility in its active-management, misfit, and excess target returns. Ruby, which limited the riskiness of its domestic equity program by its use of a modest passive-management allocation, experienced risk results between those of Diamond and Ivory.

Of particular interest are the relative magnitudes of active-management risk and misfit risk in all three programs. In each case, misfit risk was at least two-thirds the size of the active-management risk, and in the case of Diamond, misfit risk was even greater than the active-management risk. Consistent with the findings reported in Chapter 1, all of the plan sponsors were taking almost as much or more risk in an uncompensated component of return as they were in a component in which they expected to be rewarded for assuming risk.

Examining Ivory's situation more closely, we can see how a plan sponsor might respond to a developing misfit problem. At the beginning of 1987, only 33 percent of Ivory's domestic equity program was actively managed. In the absence of an extreme aggregate manager style bias, misfit was not likely to be a serious problem because of the relatively large indexed component. As indicated in Figure 4.3, in early 1987, Ivory's realized misfit was only 0.5 percent on an annualized rolling three-year basis. Two years later, Ivory began to allocate more of its assets to its active equity managers, eventually increasing the allocation to 50 percent. The rolling three-year misfit risk of the aggregate manager benchmark began to rise commensurately, creeping up toward 1 percent. Combined with the cumulatively negative misfit returns, this increase in the level of misfit risk prompted Ivory, in late 1990, to replace its target-based passive portfolio with a DCF. Excluding the index fund, of course, the non-DCF-manager misfit rose sharply. More importantly, however, Figure 4.3 shows that once the DCF was implemented, the misfit of Ivory's entire domestic equity program declined, falling below 0.5 percent by year-end 1996.

Figure 4.3. Ivory: The Effect on Misfit Risk of Implementing a DCF

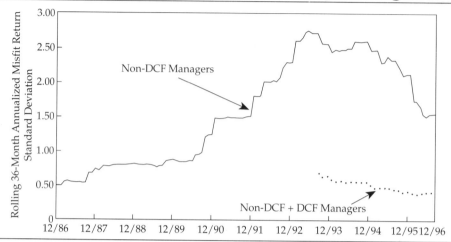

Aggregate Benchmarks and the Target in Style Space. Figure 4.4 offers a snapshot of the three plan sponsors' aggregate manager benchmarks immediately prior to the DCF deployments. The style plots all indicate the presence of misfit. The aggregate manager benchmarks were all situated in the small-cap/growth direction relative to the target. Ruby's managers displayed the most misfit, but the benchmark–target investment style divergence present in all three investment programs was sufficient to generate considerable misfit return and risk, as was demonstrated in Figures 4.1 and 4.2.

Our case study plan sponsors were not alone in experiencing significantly negative domestic equity misfit returns. The mid- and late 1980s were not kind to small-cap/growth investors. Many plan sponsors had sizable style exposures to small- and midcap/growth stocks and suffered resulting adverse impacts on their domestic equity investment results. Instead of blaming the poor relative performance of their investment programs on ineffective active management, our case study sponsors investigated further and discovered that misfit was the primary source of their problems. They then turned to a DCF as a means of mitigating that misfit.

DCF Characteristics

A DCF is dynamic because the misfit problem is dynamic. Managers are hired and fired, their benchmarks change, and even the target's composition shifts from one period to the next. Ongoing misfit control requires that the DCF be adjusted as time passes. As a result, attempting to characterize the misfit problem and the DCF solution at a point in time is difficult. Nevertheless, to

Figure 4.4. Pre-DCF Aggregate Manager Benchmarks

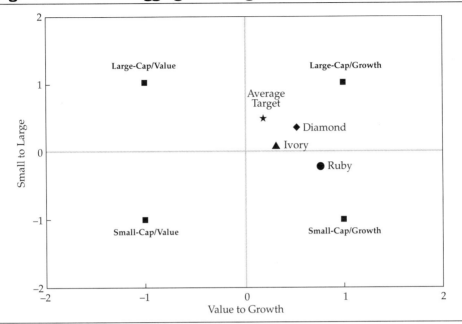

provide a sense of the basic characteristics of DCF portfolios, we examined our three plan sponsors' DCFs on a common date.

Determinants of DCF Composition. The composition of the zero-misfit DCF (and hence the constrained DCF) depends on three variables: the composition of the aggregate manager benchmark, the composition of the target, and the DCF allocation. We examined the similarities and differences in these three variables as they pertained to Diamond, Ivory, and Ruby.

All three plan sponsors chose as a target a broad market index very much like the Wilshire 5000, which is a cap-weighted index of all U.S. common stocks for which market prices are available. The sponsors' targets were so similar that they can be considered the same for purposes of our discussion.

All three plan sponsors made what we consider to be "reasonable" DCF allocations (in the range of 25–35 percent)—that is, allocations adequate to control misfit risk for a normal domestic equity manager structure without radical style biases. Given the similarities of the sponsors' targets and their DCF allocations, the differences between their DCFs were driven primarily by the investment styles of and policy allocations to their non-DCF managers.

In our experience, this situation is typical. Most sponsors select a broad market index as a target. Most also want to have as small a DCF allocation as possible, although any allocation below 25 percent can produce DCFs with unusual characteristics and extreme performance results. Sponsors often differ, however, in what their decision makers believe are the most effective combinations of investment styles and active management.

Style Positions of the Aggregate Benchmarks and the DCFs. Figure 4.5 shows the style positions of each plan sponsor's aggregate manager benchmark and the zero-misfit and constrained DCFs at the end of third-quarter 1996. As was the case prior to the DCF implementations, all three aggregate manager benchmarks, although in different locations in style space, are positioned to the southeast of the target. We believe that this location is no coincidence. The vast majority of domestic equity investment programs that we encounter display an orientation toward small-cap/growth managers. The smallness aspect is relatively easy to explain: The security-weighting schemes of most active managers resemble equal weighting much more than capitalization weighting, whereas virtually all domestic equity targets are broad capitalization-weighted market indexes. Consequently, managers find

Figure 4.5. Three Plan Sponsors' Domestic Equity Investment Programs, September 1996

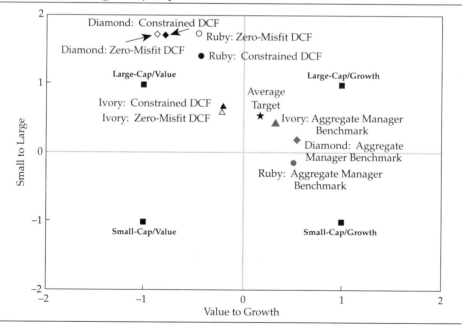

it difficult to create portfolios that have the same large-size characteristics as these targets. Even many managers that profess to follow large-cap investment styles consistently hold portfolios with a small-size bias relative to broad market indexes.

The growth tendencies of most domestic equity programs are more difficult to rationalize. We alluded to this situation in discussing Figure 1.4, when we observed the preponderance of growth managers compared with value managers. If the selection of investment styles by plan sponsors were a random process, the skewness of the manager growth/value distribution would explain the growth bias present in so many sponsors' investment programs. Because sponsors presumably take manager styles into account as they select managers and allocate funds to them, the observed growth biases are not so understandable. We are left to conclude that many sponsors view active management as more productive under a growth style than under a value style.

Ruby offers a good example of this propensity to select small-cap/growth managers. In Figure 4.6, the style graph plots not only Ruby's constrained DCF, target, and aggregate manager benchmark but also the style locations

Figure 4.6. Ruby: Detailed View of the Domestic Equity Investment Program, September 1996

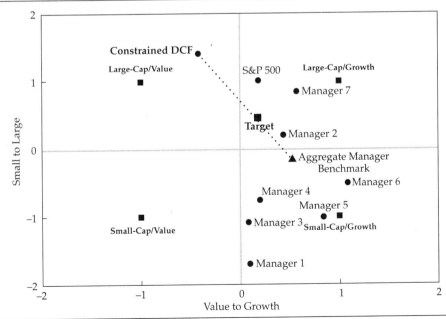

of the individual manager benchmarks. Only one manager out of seven (who represents 30 percent of the non-DCF allocation) has a benchmark with a size orientation larger than that of the target. Only two managers have a greater value orientation than the target, and four (representing 70 percent of the non-DCF allocation) have a distinctly higher growth orientation than the target. Notably, none of the managers has a large-cap/value style that would mitigate the small-cap/growth misfit evidenced by Ruby's aggregate manager benchmark.

A small-cap/growth bias in a plan sponsor's manager allocations produces a DCF portfolio that has a large-cap/value exposure. As the complement to the misfit portfolio, the DCF portfolio will have to possess large-cap/value investment characteristics if it is to effectively compensate for the small-cap/growth misfit generated by the sponsor's manager-structuring biases. Referring back to Figure 4.5, note that the style plots of the sponsors' zero-misfit and constrained DCFs show that each pair lies directly opposite the corresponding aggregate manager benchmark, relative to the position of the target.

Reflecting Ivory's fairly small active-manager allocation and misfit problem, the distance of Ivory's DCF from the target is considerably smaller than the corresponding distance for Diamond and Ruby. Diamond's DCF lies farther from the target than does Ruby's, even though its aggregate manager benchmark lies closer to the target. This difference is explained by Diamond's smaller DCF allocation.

For each plan sponsor, the zero-misfit and constrained DCFs lie very close to one another. We should expect to see this similarity in location. After all, the optimization process underlying the constrained DCF's construction is designed to produce a portfolio with the same style characteristics as those of the zero-misfit DCF, subject to any limits set on the constrained DCF's composition. In all cases, the constrained DCF is positioned less aggressively relative to the target than is the zero-misfit DCF. The restrictions placed on the construction of the constrained DCF, although necessary to produce an investable portfolio, diminish the ability of the DCF to offset the misfit of the aggregate manager benchmark. That diminution increases as the limits on the constrained DCF's composition increase.

Ivory's zero-misfit and constrained DCFs are much closer to one another than is the case for either Diamond or Ruby.[2] This positioning is again the result of the relatively smaller amount of misfit present in its investment

---

[2]The distance between Ivory's aggregate manager benchmark style plot and the target at the end of third-quarter 1996 is much less than it was at the time the DCF was implemented. This change resulted from alterations in Ivory's active-management structure (through hirings, firings, and reallocations among existing managers), which reduced the level of misfit risk.

program. The style characteristics of Ivory's zero-misfit DCF are not particularly extreme; hence, the constrained DCF has less difficulty mirroring those characteristics, even without the benefit of any short selling. On that same note, Diamond's zero-misfit and constrained DCFs are more closely situated than are Ruby's. To some extent, this pattern is the result of Diamond's less pronounced misfit problem. More important, however, is the use of short positions in Diamond's constrained DCF. In 1995, Diamond adopted a policy permitting 30 percent of its constrained DCF's invested value to be sold short. Allowing short selling increases the ability of the constrained DCF to reflect the composition of the zero-misfit DCF accurately. Figure 4.5 supports that assertion.

Financial Attributes of the Zero-Misfit and Constrained DCFs.
Table 4.1 offers another perspective on the three plan sponsors' DCFs. Listed side by side are various financial attributes of the three sets of zero-misfit and constrained DCFs. The first group in the table contains the number of stocks held in the DCFs, their weighted-average market capitalizations, the portfolios' sector weights, and their cash positions. The bottom part of the table lists selected fundamental risk factors (expressed, with the exception of beta, in standard deviation units) derived from the BARRA E2 risk model. Included in Table 4.1 as a reference are the attributes of the Wilshire 5000 Index.

A comparison of the DCFs, both among the plan sponsors and against the target, in Table 4.1 displays some striking differences. In general, all of the DCFs have a large-cap/low-growth bias relative to the target, reflecting the small-cap/growth styles of the sponsors' active managers. Because of their more aggressive structuring of active managers, Diamond's and Ruby's aggregate manager benchmarks have much more misfit than does Ivory's. As a result, the zero-misfit DCFs of Diamond and Ruby have more-extreme attribute exposures relative to the target than does Ivory, especially among the size and growth attributes and in certain sectors, such as consumer nondurables and energy.

The constrained DCFs provide some interesting comparisons with the zero-misfit DCFs. As should be the case, the constrained DCFs contain similar attribute exposures relative to the target as their corresponding zero-misfit DCFs, but those relative exposures are generally less pronounced than those of the zero-misfit DCFs. Diamond's constrained DCF appears to be much more like the zero-misfit DCF than does Ruby's. The reason is Diamond's inclusion of short positions in its constrained DCF. Indeed, the technology weighting in Diamond's constrained DCF is actually negative.

The difference in cash positions of the DCFs merits mention. The plan sponsors differ on their policies toward the use of cash in manager benchmarks and the target. Ivory allows no cash in any manager benchmarks or the

Table 4.1. DCF Characteristics, September 1996

Characteristic	Diamond		Ivory		Ruby		Wilshire 5000
	Zero-Misfit DCF	Constrained DCF	Zero-Misfit DCF	Constrained DCF	Zero-Misfit DCF	Constrained DCF	
Stocks (number)	5,345	2,244	7,386	1,821	6,308	636	7,167
Average market cap (millions)	$49,662	$47,885	$33,042	$30,068	$48,288	$40,649	$23,583
Sector							
Consumer nondurables	12.90%	12.22%	28.95%	27.93%	20.62%	20.46%	37.70%
Consumer durables	2.89	3.01	2.65	3.03	-1.71	3.02	3.55
Basic materials	13.51	9.35	8.75	8.89	10.17	8.42	7.72
Capital goods	7.93	6.59	7.10	6.91	3.75	5.07	7.10
Energy	17.04	20.84	9.22	8.55	14.54	20.03	5.98
Technology	-8.41	-1.95	4.24	4.75	5.85	3.96	9.01
Transportation	1.87	0.44	1.27	1.64	1.78	0.51	1.88
Utilities	23.72	26.89	16.04	16.54	19.56	23.72	10.09
Financials	28.55	22.61	21.78	21.76	25.44	14.81	16.97
Cash	7.31	7.31	0.00	0.00	-0.91	0.50	0.00
Risk factors (units of standard deviation[a])							
Success	-0.32	-0.26	-0.09	-0.09	-0.17	-0.13	0.01
Size	1.21	1.09	-0.18	-0.07	1.25	0.62	-0.38
Growth	-1.04	-0.99	-0.24	-0.27	-0.84	-0.58	0.11
Earnings/price	0.47	0.46	0.10	0.13	0.34	0.21	-0.04
Book/price	0.30	0.31	0.16	0.16	0.15	0.15	0.02
Earnings variability	-0.36	-0.41	-0.06	-0.06	-0.43	-0.27	0.07
Yield	0.93	0.99	0.28	0.30	0.72	0.68	-0.08
Beta	0.72×	0.75×	0.89×	0.90×	0.79×	0.87×	1.00×

[a]Except beta.

target. As a result, its DCF contains no cash because cash misfit effectively has been defined away. Both Diamond and Ruby allow the managers' benchmarks to reflect the managers' tendencies to hold cash. In Diamond's case, the target has a larger cash allocation than the aggregate manager benchmark, producing a negative cash misfit and, therefore, a positive DCF cash position. Ruby faces just the opposite situation.

DCF Results

How have our three plan sponsors' DCFs actually performed? To better understand the answer, we examined the issue from the perspective of the various alternative misfit-control measures discussed in Chapter 2. This analysis offers insights into the relative magnitude of misfit control these alternatives provide. In particular, we expected the DCF solution to produce superior misfit control compared with the other alternatives. Do the actual DCF results conform to these expectations, and to what extent do the alternatives reduce misfit? Specifically, we considered the performance of the

- aggregate manager benchmark (Misfit Solution 1);
- aggregate manager benchmark plus an index fund based on the asset category target (Misfit Solution 6);
- aggregate manager benchmark plus a combination of style indexes designed to correct the misfit (Misfit Solution 7);
- aggregate manager benchmark plus the DCF portfolio composed of constrained security positions: the constrained DCF (Misfit Solution 10); and
- aggregate manager benchmark plus the DCF portfolio composed of unconstrained long and short security positions: the zero-misfit DCF (Misfit Solution 9).

Performance of the Misfit-Control Alternatives. Figure 4.7 summarizes the comparative misfit-control analysis.[3] The performance of each alternative is presented in clusters composed of the three plan sponsors' results from the inception of their DCFs through September 30, 1996. Although the amount of misfit each sponsor experienced varies, the results viewed across the set of alternative misfit-control methods are essentially uniform and monotonically decreasing as we move from the "do-nothing" option all the way to the zero-misfit DCF option.

Ruby clearly presented the most difficult misfit problem. The misfit risk

---

[3] For each alternative (except the first), the returns of the misfit-control portfolio under analysis were combined with the aggregate manager benchmark's returns, proportional to the DCF and the non-DCF allocations, respectively. Returns were calculated monthly, and any changes in the DCF's allocation during the period of analysis were accounted for in the combined return.

Figure 4.7. Performance of Various Misfit-Control Alternatives

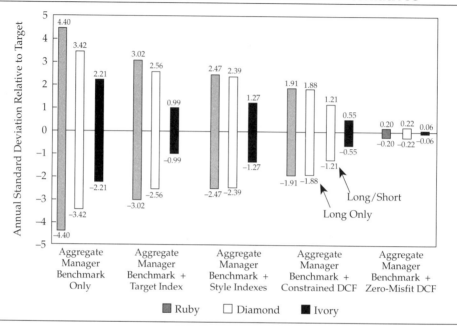

of its aggregate manager benchmark alone exceeded 4 percent a year. Even Ivory's non-DCF manager misfit risk was greater than 2 percent annually.

Combining an index fund invested in the target with the aggregate manager benchmark reduced misfit risk by roughly 25 percent for Ruby and Diamond. Ivory's misfit declined more than 50 percent. In all cases, the data show that shifting weight to the center of the boat does indeed produce misfit-control benefits.

The use of combined-style portfolios reduced misfit risk even further for Ruby and Diamond, but not for Ivory. When aggregate manager style biases are large, the ability of the combined-style solution to adjust to the unique aspects of a plan sponsor's misfit problem can be very advantageous. This solution suffers, however, from nonmarket risk caused by the style portfolios' concentrations in particular industries and securities. In the case of a plan sponsor such as Ivory, which already has a relatively low level of misfit risk, the highly diversified (although inflexible) nature of the index fund solution can outperform the nonmarket risk-laden (but highly flexible) nature of the combined-style solution.

The two DCF solutions yielded the most effective misfit-risk control. Directly addressing each plan sponsor's unique misfit problem on a stock-by-stock basis brought considerably more misfit-risk reduction than any of the other alternatives. The constrained DCF solution reduced misfit risk by more than 50 percent in all cases. The zero-misfit DCF solution pushed misfit risk down to almost negligible levels.

Diamond's decision to permit some short selling in its constrained DCF provides additional insights into the potential misfit-control benefits of the DCF solution. Previously, the constrained DCF, when combined with Diamond's aggregate manager benchmark, produced annualized misfit risk of 1.88 percent (a 45 percent misfit-risk reduction); the inclusion of some short positions resulted in misfit risk of only 1.21 percent (a 65 percent misfit-risk reduction) for the brief period of time that the new policy has been in effect. We expect (and the data in Figure 4.7 lend support to that expectation) that allowing short selling to the modest extent permitted by Diamond can result in misfit reductions of up to 75 percent, as opposed to the 50 percent reduction experienced with long-only constrained DCFs.

Reconciling the DCF's Performance. A plan sponsor implementing a DCF will want to periodically reconcile its investment program's misfit return and the DCF's performance. The DCF builder should be responsible for regularly reporting on the progress of the misfit-control effort. Using Ruby as an example, Table 4.2 shows how such a monthly reporting format might be prepared. The table displays the allocations to, and the performance of, each of Ruby's manager benchmarks during one month.[4] Those benchmark returns are weighted by the managers' policy allocations to produce a non-DCF-manager benchmark return.

The non-DCF-manager benchmark return is joined with the zero-misfit DCF's return and the constrained DCF's return, according to the respective non-DCF and DCF allocations. This combined return is compared with the target's return to measure the misfit remaining in the program after application of the DCF. In this particular month, the non-DCF-manager benchmark return was 0.42 percent and the target returned 1.48 percent. With a 33 percent DCF allocation, the misfit associated with the zero-misfit DCF was –0.01 percent; the misfit was 0.18 percent with the constrained DCF. Accumulating these data consistently over time provides the information necessary to evaluate the DCF's effectiveness.

Correlation between the Constrained DCF and Aggregate Manager Benchmark Returns Relative to the Target. Appendix B demonstrates that on an *ex ante* basis, the zero-misfit DCF return relative to the target should be

---

[4]Note the wide variation in the benchmark performance among Ruby's managers—more than 400 bps in one month. This return spread re-emphasizes the tremendous potential impact of manager investment styles on the investment program's performance.

Table 4.2.   Ruby: DCF Return Reconciliation, December 1995

Manager	Policy Weight	Benchmark Equity-Only Return	Benchmark Cash	Total Benchmark Return
1	3.0%	2.36%	5.0%	2.27%
2	10.0	0.95	5.0	0.92
3	5.0	2.22	5.0	2.13
4	12.0	0.70	10.0	0.67
5	5.0	2.87	8.0	2.68
6	12.0	−1.93	15.0	−1.58
7	20.0	−0.08	5.0	−0.06
Non-DCF managers	67.0%	0.42%	7.9%	0.42%
Target	100.0	1.54	5.0	1.48
Zero-misfit DCF	33.0	3.60	−0.9	3.63
Overall program misfit				−0.01
Constrained DCF	33.0	4.20	0.5	4.18
Overall program misfit				0.18

perfectly negatively correlated with the aggregate manager benchmark's misfit return; that is,

$$\rho\,[(B^* - T),\,(B_{DCF} - T)] = -1.$$

Also, the standard deviation of the zero-misfit DCF's return relative to the target is related to the standard deviation of the active-manager benchmark's misfit by a factor of $(1 - w_{DCF})/w_{DCF}$, where w_{DCF} is the DCF allocation. Consequently, if we graphed the returns of the aggregate manager benchmark and the zero-misfit DCF, both relative to the return of the target, we should observe mirror images moving in exactly the opposite directions, although the DCF's relative returns have greater amplitude than the aggregate manager benchmark's relative returns.

By the nature of its construction, the constrained DCF will not exactly replicate the performance of the zero-misfit DCF. As a result, the constrained DCF return net of the target's return will not be perfectly negatively correlated with non-DCF-managers' aggregate misfit return. The realized correlation, however, should be quite close to −1. *Ex post*, the correlation provides a quick (although hardly complete) test of the constrained DCF's effectiveness.

The negative relationship between the constrained DCF and the aggregate manager benchmark is evidenced by Diamond's historical DCF performance, shown in Figure 4.8. When the non-DCF managers' benchmarks have underperformed the target, the constrained DCF has taken up the slack by exceeding the target's return. The converse also has held true. In fact, for this period, the correlation between the two relative return series was −0.88. The misfit of the entire domestic equity program, shown by the dotted line in Figure 4.8, is thus much less volatile and of a much smaller magnitude than either the DCF's or the aggregate manager benchmark's returns relative to the target.

Figure 4.8. Diamond: Return Correlation of the Constrained DCF and the Aggregate Manager Benchmark, June 1989–December 1996

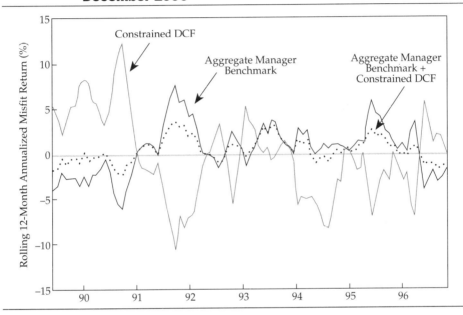

5. A Utility-Based Perspective on DCFs

A comparison of the advantages and disadvantages of the DCF relative to alternative misfit-control approaches indicates that it is the logical solution to the misfit problem. In this chapter, we consider the DCF's relative benefits from a more theoretical perspective. Specifically, we demonstrate that a plan sponsor can enhance the utility expected from a multiple-active-manager investment program by implementing a DCF.

The Plan Sponsor's Utility

From the plan sponsor's point of view, utility is a nebulous term. Economics textbooks define utility as "satisfaction." In general, utility defies easy quantification. Measuring the utility that a plan sponsor derives from its investment program is particularly difficult. Unlike an individual investor, a sponsor represents a potentially large number of stakeholders. These stakeholders may range from plan beneficiaries, such as retired pensioners who desire security for their benefit payments, to corporate executives, who may be sensitive to the earnings ramifications of a pension fund's results. Despite these difficulties, we will operate under the pretext that the sponsor is a single entity whose utility is affected in a straightforward way by the performance of the plan's investment program.

Assume that the plan sponsor's expected utility (hereafter, simply utility) is a function of both its total portfolio (i.e., all of its investments within an asset category, which we designate as N^*) and the asset category target, T. The utility the sponsor derives by holding N^* instead of T is $U(N^*, T)$. For a specific asset category, the target is the single portfolio the sponsor would prefer to hold in the absence of all active management. For our purposes, then, T is neutral in terms of utility, with $U(T, T) = 0$. In designing an actively managed investment program using multiple managers, the sponsor expects to generate favorable outcomes relative to T; that is, the sponsor intends to outperform T on a risk-adjusted basis, resulting in $U(N^*, T) > 0$.

Just as any portfolio can be separated into benchmark and value-added components $(P = B + A)$, a plan sponsor's utility derived from a manager's portfolio also can be divided into two parts: the utility contributed by the benchmark and the utility contributed by the value-added component of the manager's portfolio. Thus,

$$U(B + A, T) = U(A, 0) + U(B, T). \tag{5.1}$$

Note that the "target" for the value-added component is zero. This designation indicates that the value-added component of a portfolio is a hedge portfolio; effectively, the alternative to holding the value-added component is to hold a null portfolio.

The Allocation to the DCF

Does a plan sponsor achieve the greatest utility by allocating all of its funds to the one or two managers expected to produce the largest values added? Of course, the answer is no. Such a strategy is analogous to a manager investing his or her entire portfolio in the single asset with the highest expected return. Instead, the sponsor will diversify among managers, just as the managers diversify among assets. This diversification controls the sponsor's total portfolio risk.

In Equation 2.3, let w_i denote an individual manager's weight in the total portfolio or the fraction of total assets that the plan sponsor chooses to allocate to its ith manager. Because managers, in practice, cannot be "shorted," each manager's weight is non-negative ($w_i \geq 0$). The aggregate fraction of the plan sponsor's total portfolio assigned to its non-DCF managers is the sum of those managers' weights, w_{mgrs}. If the sponsor gives all of its assets to the non-DCF managers, then $w_{mgrs} = 1$. We assume that sponsors do not borrow money in order to fund their non-DCF managers, so $w_{mgrs} \leq 1$.

The plan sponsor's aggregate manager portfolio, P^*, is the sum of the non-DCF managers' portfolios multiplied by their respective weights in the total portfolio. We define the aggregate manager benchmark, B^*, and the aggregate manager value-added portfolio, A^*, similarly. As a result, the sum of the aggregate manager benchmark and the aggregate manager value-added portfolio is the aggregate manager portfolio:

$$P^* = B^* + A^*. \tag{5.2}$$

The weight of the aggregate manager benchmark, B^*, equals the weight of the aggregate manager portfolio, P^*, which equals w_{mgrs}, the sum of the non-DCF manager weights. Again, the aggregate manager value-added portfolio, A^*, is a hedge portfolio with zero net weight.

The plan sponsor may not give all of its assets to its non-DCF managers, or it may give all of its assets to those managers but invest in a hedge portfolio in addition to the non-DCF manager holdings. In either case, there will be a portfolio of DCF manager holdings, which we have labeled H. With N^* defined as the plan sponsor's total portfolio, by including the non-DCF managers' holdings and those of the DCF manager, we can write

$$N^* = P^* + H. \tag{5.3}$$

Recall that in Misfit Solution 9, H was defined as a hedge portfolio called the zero-misfit dynamic completeness fund. In the context of the current discussion, H is the portion of the plan sponsor's assets not invested with the non-DCF managers. It is the difference between the sponsor's total portfolio, N^*, and the aggregate non-DCF manager portfolio, P^*. Depending on how the sponsor allocates assets to the non-DCF managers, H may or may not be a hedge portfolio. In general, the weight of H is $1 - w_{mgrs}$.

Value-Added Utility and Tracking Disutility

We now examine the dynamic completeness fund, H, more closely from the perspective of the plan sponsor's utility. Because H is the portion of the sponsor's assets not controlled by the non-DCF managers, the sponsor cannot use the information contained in the value-added portfolios, A_i, to choose H. Presumably, the managers would take a dim view of their skills being used without compensation, so we assume that the sponsor creates H using publicly available information; that is, it forms H as a linear combination of the non-DCF managers' benchmarks and the asset category target, T, such that $H = T - B^*$.

Using Equations 5.2 and 5.3, we can rewrite the plan sponsor's utility function as

$$U(N^*, T) = U(B^* + A^* + H, T).$$

Equivalently,

$$U(N^*, T) = U(A^*, 0) + U(B^* + H, T). \tag{5.4}$$

Equation 5.4 states that the plan sponsor's utility is the sum of two distinct parts: the utility of the value added, which depends on manager selection, and the misfit present in the sponsor's total portfolio or the ability of the aggregate manager benchmark and DCF combination to track the performance of the target. This second utility component can be viewed as the tracking disutility, which depends on manager selection and on the allocation to and composition of the DCF.

The target must have the property that $U(X, T) \leq 0$ for any Portfolio X that does not include manager value-added information. (If this relationship does not hold, the target has been inappropriately selected.) Because the aggregate manager benchmark and the dynamic completeness fund do not include manager value-added information, the tracking disutility term, $U(B^* + H, T)$, is, at best, zero (which is why we call it disutility rather than utility).

We expect the non-DCF managers to add value and the DCF to correct any problems that the plan sponsor confronts when constructing a portfolio of multiple managers. That is, we expect that $U(A^*, 0) > 0$ and seek H with $U(B^* + H, T)$ equal to zero (or not very negative).[1] If the non-DCF managers do not add utility (that is, if $U[A^*, 0] \leq 0$ for all choices of the manager weights), then the plan sponsor can achieve maximum utility by forgoing all active management (setting $w_{mgrs} = 0$) and investing passively in the target. When the active managers do add value, H "completes" the sponsor's portfolio by reducing tracking disutility.

As defined in Equation 2.3, the misfit in a plan sponsor's portfolio is the difference between its aggregate manager benchmark and its asset category target; that is, misfit equals $B^* - T$. Equation 2.4 defined the misfit-correcting portfolio, H, as $T - B^*$. If the sponsor establishes H as its DCF, the sponsor will eliminate disutility no matter what manager weights are chosen. The sponsor can now proceed in two steps: It first chooses the set of manager weights that maximizes the utility of value added and then eliminates tracking disutility by implementing the dynamic completeness fund.

The DCF removes the misfit between the aggregate manager benchmark and the target. It does so without interfering with the value added by the non-DCF managers because it does not affect the manager weights that determine the utility of the value added. In fact, the active managers' actual portfolios are not even considered in forming the misfit-correcting portfolio. They go about constructing their portfolios oblivious to the composition of the DCF.

Other Issues

The DCF accounts for a fraction of the plan sponsor's total portfolio. Thus, the difference between the weight of the long component of the DCF and the weight of the short component is $1 - w_{mgrs}$. One way a plan sponsor can address its concerns about short selling is to limit the size of the short positions so that their total weight is, at most, some fraction, c. Many sponsors require that c equal zero, so their DCFs contain no short positions at all. In Chapter 2, we referred to a limited short-selling DCF as a constrained DCF.

When should a plan sponsor consider implementing a DCF? If the tracking disutility for the sponsor is only slightly negative, the sponsor's total portfolio will exhibit adequate manager diversification and the sponsor will

---

[1]Because $U(T, T) = 0$, setting $B^* + H$ equal to T will maximize this misfit component of utility. If the proxy for H (say, the constrained DCF) results in $B^* + H \neq T$, then the misfit component of utility will be negative.

not benefit materially by implementing a DCF. If the sponsor's tracking disutility is significantly negative, however, some action is required. We believe that most sponsors perceive misfit-risk levels above 1 percent per annum standard deviation to produce meaningful disutility. In such cases, we contend that the DCF offers the most effective means of controlling misfit risk and simultaneously maximizing the utility of the value added.

Some plan sponsors attempt to control misfit risk by allocating a portion of their assets to an index fund (Misfit Solution 6). In this case, $w_{mgrs} < 1$, and the plan sponsor invests the nonactive manager portion of its portfolio in the target. Mathematically, the sponsor has substituted $(1 - w_{mgrs})T$ for H in Equation 5.4. This solution may reduce tracking disutility to acceptable levels. In general, however, it will always be more desirable to have a DCF in place than to use an index fund because the set of DCFs includes index funds; in fact, index funds are but one example—and a very restricted example, at that—of dynamic completeness funds. DCFs, with or without restrictions on short sales, are always as good as or better than index funds from the perspective of sponsor utility.

6. Advanced DCF Concepts

Our focus so far has been on the participants and steps involved in constructing a dynamic completeness fund. Now, we turn to several more-advanced DCF concepts. Those readers not wishing to become immersed in DCF details can skip this material, without loss of continuity, and move directly to Chapter 7.

Zero-Misfit DCF: Zero and Plus-NAV Versions

Up to this point, we have defined the zero-misfit DCF as a hedge portfolio that satisfies the condition that $H = T - B^*$. This equation expresses the DCF concept in its simplest and most efficient form. For every security contained in either the target or the aggregate manager benchmark but not held at the same weight in both portfolios, a nonzero position in that security exists in H. Securities overweighted in the target relative to the aggregate manager benchmark are held in H as positive positions, and securities relatively underweighted in the target become negative positions in H. The resulting portfolio, if combined with the aggregate manager benchmark, will yield the target (i.e., $H + B^* = T$) and, therefore, eliminate all misfit.

The weights of the securities contained in H can be expressed in dollars or in percentages. In either case, the sum of those weights is zero. Henceforth, using net asset value (NAV), we will refer to the hedge portfolio that eliminates misfit in the plan sponsor's investment program by the tongue-twisting term *zero-NAV/zero-misfit DCF*.

The zero-misfit DCF need not be a hedge portfolio. Once we drop the zero-NAV requirement for the zero-misfit DCF, we force a decision on the plan sponsor. The sponsor must choose how much of the total investment program to assign to the non-DCF managers (which we call w_{mgrs}) and how much to allocate to the DCF (which we call w_{DCF}). Because the allocations to the non-DCF managers and the DCF must sum to 1, $w_{DCF} = 1 - w_{mgrs}$.

This relationship leads to a more general specification of the zero-misfit DCF, namely, that

$$H = T - (1 - w_{DCF})B^*. \tag{6.1}$$

When $w_{DCF} = 0$, the plan sponsor has assigned all its assets to the non-DCF managers and H has no net assets. Conversely, when $w_{DCF} > 0$, a portion of the investment program has been placed in the zero-misfit DCF. The zero-misfit DCF is no longer a hedge portfolio; it now has a positive net asset value.

In this case, we refer to the DCF as a *plus-NAV/zero-misfit DCF*.

The choice of a DCF allocation has direct ramifications for the misfit problem. Assigning a portion of the investment program, w_{DCF}, to the DCF dilutes the misfit associated with the aggregate manager benchmark and, therefore, affects the characteristics of the zero-misfit DCF. At the extreme, when $w_{DCF} = 1$, then $H = T$; the plan sponsor uses no non-DCF managers, and consequently, the investment program has no misfit. The zero-misfit DCF is merely an index fund invested in the target.

From our perspective, of course, the more relevant situation involves a group of non-DCF managers and an aggregate manager benchmark that differs from the target (i.e., $T \neq B^*$). Under those conditions, changing the DCF allocation alters H. We can illustrate this effect by referring back to Table 1.3. Assume that the plan sponsor's investment program has a total value of $100.00 and that the sponsor decides to allocate 10 percent (or $10.00) of the program's assets to the DCF. As shown in Table 6.1, the dollar investments in each of the 10 securities in the target are found by multiplying their investment proportions in Table 1.3 by $100.00. Similarly, the dollar investment in each of the aggregate manager benchmark securities is found by multiplying $90.00 ($100.00 × 0.9) by the benchmark securities' respective investment proportions.

The zero-misfit DCF ($H = T - [1 - w_{DCF}]B^*$) in dollar terms is found by subtracting the benchmark's invested dollars from those of the target. In total, $10.00 is invested in the plus-NAV/zero-misfit DCF. The long component's value is +$51.80, and the short component's value is –$41.80. As an exercise, the reader can calculate the composition of the plus-NAV/zero-misfit DCF if the plan sponsor assigns it a $20.00 (or 20 percent) allocation. The long side

Table 6.1. Example of a Plus-NAV/Zero-Misfit DCF

Security	Non-DCF Benchmark Holdings	Asset Category Target Holdings	Plus-NAV/Zero-Misfit DCF Holdings
1	$18.90	$13.00	–$5.90
2	0.00	9.00	+9.00
3	21.60	15.00	–6.60
4	27.00	6.00	–21.00
5	0.00	5.00	+5.00
6	0.00	16.00	+16.00
7	0.00	8.00	+8.00
8	7.20	11.00	+3.80
9	0.00	10.00	+10.00
10	15.30	7.00	–8.30
Total	$90.00	$100.00	$10.00

of the DCF will then have a value of +$52.60, and the short side's value will be
–$32.60.

With the plus-NAV/zero-misfit DCF, expressing security weights
becomes an issue. Stated in dollars, the total weight of the portfolio is no longer
zero; instead, it is some positive value equal to the w_{DCF} times the value of the
entire investment program. Stated in percentages, the sum of the security
weights is w_{DCF}. Managers and plan sponsors, however, are used to thinking
in terms of portfolios, in which the percentage weights total 1, or 100 percent.
To accommodate this convention, we introduce an additional term, B_{DCF},
which is the plus-NAV/zero-misfit DCF with security weights normalized so
as to sum to 1; that is,

$$B_{DCF} = \frac{H}{w_{DCF}}.$$

In general, then, the plus-NAV/zero-misfit DCF is the portfolio B_{DCF} that
solves

$$T - (1 - w_{DCF})B^* - w_{DCF} B_{DCF} = 0,$$

or equivalently,

$$H = w_{DCF}B_{DCF}$$
$$= T - (1 - w_{DCF}) B^*. \tag{6.2}$$

Equation 6.2 specifies the exact composition of the plus-NAV/zero-misfit DCF
given the compositions of and allocations to the m non-DCF managers'
benchmarks and the composition of the target.

Impracticality of Owning the Zero-Misfit DCF

To fully replicate the zero-misfit DCF, the DCF manager would create a
portfolio that is the exact complement of the misfit portfolio $(B^* - T)$. From
an execution standpoint, the DCF manager is concerned with the number of
securities in which he or she must transact and the size of those transactions,
particularly on the short side of the portfolio.

Number of Zero-Misfit DCF Securities. The seriousness of these concerns depends on the composition of the target and manager benchmarks and
on the size of the plan sponsor's investment program. Every security that is
misfit (i.e., the security's weight in the target does not match its weight in the
aggregate manager benchmark) will be held in either a long or a short position
in the zero-misfit DCF.[1] The worst case for the DCF manager occurs when

---

[1] Note that this statement applies to both the zero-NAV and plus-NAV versions of the DCF.

the target and the aggregate manager benchmark are completely disjoint (i.e., the portfolios share no securities). In that situation, the number of securities in the zero-misfit DCF will equal the sum of the number of securities in the target plus the number in the aggregate manager benchmark. Securities in the target will be held as long positions, and securities in the aggregate manager benchmark will be sold short. Given that a broad domestic equity market index, such as the Wilshire 5000, contains more than 7,000 stocks, this worst full-replication case would involve transacting in a hopelessly large number of stocks.

Of course, the best full-replication case occurs when the target and the aggregate manager benchmark contain exactly the same securities and hold those securities in exactly the same proportions. In that situation, if $w_{DCF} = 0$, both the misfit portfolio and the zero-misfit DCF are null; otherwise, if $w_{DCF} > 0$, the zero-misfit DCF is equivalent to the target.

Assuming that the target is a broad market index, the most likely case falls somewhere in between the two extremes; that is, the aggregate manager benchmark constitutes a subset of the target, but the weights of most securities in the two portfolios differ. In that situation, the number of securities in the zero-misfit DCF will equal that of the target less the few zero-misfit securities. If the target includes many more securities than the aggregate manager benchmark (which is often, but not always, the case), then the number of long positions will far exceed the number of short positions.

Table 6.2 gives a sense of the number of securities in typical plus-NAV/zero-misfit DCFs and the relative proportions assigned to the long and short components. Each sponsor has selected an extended domestic equity market index, such as the Wilshire 5000, as its target. The DCFs are shown in the normalized form (B_{DCF}) so that the security weights sum to 1. The DCF allocations run from roughly 10 percent to 45 percent. In absolute value, the short positions generally range from 15 percent to 75 percent of the DCF's

Table 6.2. Several Plan Sponsors' Zero-Misfit DCFs, December 1996

Plan Sponsor	Long Side		Short Side		Total Stocks	DCF Weight
	Weight	Number of Stocks	Weight	Number of Stocks		
Diamond	172.36%	2,488	72.36%	2,982	5,470	27.90%
Feldspar	174.80	2,356	74.80	693	3,049	30.00
Gold	113.21	3,102	13.21	606	3,708	43.80
Ivory	115.89	6,634	15.89	712	7,346	27.55
Ruby	163.62	4,015	63.62	2,312	6,327	33.00
Uranium	400.01	2,871	300.01	774	3,645	12.50

total invested position. The plan sponsor Uranium is the exception. Its DCF allocation is relatively small, and the style biases of its managers are relatively large; therefore, it has a much larger short position than is typical.

Amount of Dollars Invested in the Zero-Misfit DCF. The dollar amount invested in the zero-misfit DCF's long and short positions can also be viewed from the extremes. At one end of the spectrum is the situation in which the target and aggregate manager benchmark are completely disjoint. For the zero-NAV/zero-misfit DCF, the absolute values of the long and the short components are equivalent; therefore, the sum of the absolute values of the long and short components will be *twice* the size of the entire investment program. For example, a $1 billion domestic equity program will hold $1 billion long of target securities and $1 billion short of aggregate manager benchmark securities. In the case of the plus-NAV/zero-misfit DCF, the long component will be greater than the short component in absolute value, with the difference depending on w_{DCF}. The larger the w_{DCF}, the less the combined absolute values of the long and short components.

At the opposite end of the spectrum, when the target and the aggregate manager benchmark completely overlap and no securities are misfit, the amounts invested in the long and short components of the zero-NAV/zero-misfit DCF each equal zero. For the plus-NAV version, the short component will have no value and the long component will equal w_{DCF} times the size of the investment program, with each constituent security's weight proportional to its position in the target.

In between these polar cases, the amount invested in the long and short components is calculated by multiplying each long or short percentage position by the dollar amount held in the investment program. The more extreme the misfit positions, the larger the absolute value of the security positions in the short component; that is, the larger the overweight position of a security in the aggregate manager benchmark relative to its weight in the target, the larger the short position of the security in the zero-misfit DCF. Assuming, however, that the smallest holding in the aggregate manager benchmark is zero, long positions in the zero-misfit DCF will never be greater than the securities' respective weights in the target.

For these reasons, buying the long side of the zero-misfit DCF should present no greater execution problems for the DCF manager than investing in a standard broad market index fund. Selling the short side, however, could present serious implementation problems, particularly if many of the plan sponsor's managers follow the same illiquid names. These problems are magnified as the size of the sponsor's investment program increases and the DCF allocation decreases.

DCF Slippage

The zero-misfit DCF removes all misfit *ex ante* from an investment program. In reality, however, DCF management would never be able to eliminate all misfit *ex post*, even if the DCF manager could invest directly in the zero-misfit DCF at no cost. Although the misfit would be very small (only a few basis points a year), it would still not be completely abolished. We call this residual misfit *DCF slippage*.

Slippage has four causes. First, the DCF is built *before* the beginning of an evaluation period by using publicly available information known at that time. This procedure allows the DCF manager to inspect the benchmark before actually being held accountable for its performance. Between the time the DCF is constructed and the start of the evaluation period, however, the weights of securities in any manager benchmarks that are rebalanced less frequently than the DCF may shift because of changes in their relative prices. (For example, the DCF may be rebalanced quarterly, but some benchmarks may be rebalanced semiannually.) These uncontrollable security-weighting changes cause the DCF to be slightly misspecified at the beginning of the evaluation period. If a published market index used as the target (or as one of the non-DCF managers' benchmarks) is changed after the DCF is constructed but before the start of the evaluation period, DCF misspecification will also occur. In addition, managers may deliver incorrect benchmarks to the DCF builder. If those benchmarks are corrected after the rebalanced DCF has become effective (i.e., after the start of the evaluation period), the DCF will have been misspecified.

The second reason for DCF slippage is a subtle mathematical quirk: After the first period in which returns are calculated (returns are usually computed on a monthly basis) and before the next DCF rebalancing, the aggregate manager benchmark's return generally will not equal the weighted sum of the individual manager benchmark returns; that is, $(1 - w_{DCF})B^* \neq \sum w_j B_j$ after the first performance-measurement period. This situation occurs because of security price drift in the various benchmarks. Within each manager's benchmark, an individual security's weight changes as its market price changes *relative* to the other securities in the benchmark. For any given security, that relative change almost certainly will be slightly different across all the manager benchmarks from the relative change that occurs in the aggregate manager benchmark and, therefore, in the zero-misfit DCF. *Ex post* misfit is usually computed by comparing the weighted sum of all the non-DCF managers' benchmarks against the DCF, not by comparing the aggregate manager benchmark against the DCF—thus the slippage.

The third reason for slippage is securities within the aggregate manager benchmark or target that cease trading as a result of takeovers or bankruptcy. These securities are removed from the portfolios for return-calculation purposes. Their weights are effectively redistributed among all the other securities in the portfolio on a pro rata basis. Similar to the second reason, this redistribution takes place across the affected individual manager benchmarks slightly differently from the way it takes effect in the target or DCF.

The final reason for slippage is differences in return-calculation methodologies. Returns reported by vendors of various market indexes may differ from the returns calculated for the same indexes by the DCF builder or other performance-measurement organizations. In the ideal situation, all parties would compute the same return on a portfolio with unambiguously specified constituents and associated weights. In reality, that is not the case. For example, some organizations calculate returns assuming dividends are paid on the ex-date (an unrealistic assumption, we might add); others use the payable date. These methodological differences can cause slippage if the sponsor insists on using a vendor's reported return for a target but uses an organization with a different return-calculation algorithm to compute the returns on the aggregate manager benchmark and DCF.

Table 6.3 depicts the realized misfit tracking error produced by the plus-NAV/zero-misfit DCFs of five plan sponsors for the three-year period ending December 31, 1996. The misfit return standard deviations shown in the table are entirely out-of-sample results after including all the sources of DCF slippage. Although the level of misfit risk is small (in all cases, 0.20 percent a year or less), it is not zero. We believe these figures represent, in a real sense, the absolute lower limits to misfit-risk reduction.

Why Not Ignore the Zero-Misfit DCF?

The zero-misfit DCF, either the zero-NAV or plus-NAV version, presents considerable difficulties from the perspective of creating an investable DCF portfolio. It contains potentially thousands of securities, a large portion of

Table 6.3. Realized Total Misfit Risk Using a Zero-Misfit DCF, 1994–96

Plan Sponsor	Annualized Misfit Standard Deviation
Diamond	0.20%
Gold	0.06
Ivory	0.07
Ruby	0.20
Uranium	0.12

which will be sold short. Many of the short positions will be in small, relatively illiquid securities for which executing short sales will be a problem. Even if a plan sponsor were able to construct and maintain the zero-misfit DCF at no cost, it would still not be able to eliminate all misfit because of the slippages inherent in the construction process and performance-measurement methods. Therefore, although the zero-misfit DCF is *measurable*, in reality it is *uninvestable*. We might seem justified in ignoring it and moving straight to the constrained DCF, which would seem to have more relevance for DCF managers.

Actually, the zero-misfit DCF is central to the entire DCF construction process. Because it offers the maximum level of misfit-risk control, it serves as the baseline for evaluating more-practical efforts. By analogy, the Wilshire 5000 is impossible to replicate fully, yet many organizations construct portfolios designed to mirror its performance. Those portfolio returns rarely match the index's return in any given month or quarter (in fact, they generally exhibit standard deviations around the index of 50–60 bps a year), but to argue that the Wilshire 5000 is uninvestable, thus irrelevant, misses the point. It reflects the performance of virtually the entire publicly traded U.S. stock market. As such, it provides an important reference for practitioners desiring to create broad investable market benchmarks.

The zero-misfit DCF is also valuable because it offers insights into the problems the DCF builder faces. He or she must create a portfolio that replicates the performance of the zero-misfit DCF within acceptable tolerances but is realistically constrained so as to yield an investable benchmark for the DCF manager. Examining the ratio of long- to short-position values in the zero-misfit DCF gives an indication of how difficult it will be to produce an effective investable approximation. The lower the ratio, the more short selling takes place in the zero-misfit DCF and, therefore, the more "work" the constrained DCF will have to perform to adequately track the zero-misfit DCF's returns.

The DCF builder should monitor the performance of the zero-misfit DCF to verify that "ground zero" on an *ex ante* basis is nearly ground zero on an *ex post* basis. The DCF builder should supply the plan sponsor and the DCF manager with estimates of the constrained DCF's ability to track the returns of the zero-misfit DCF. Doing so prior to the start of an evaluation period provides interested parties with the information necessary to monitor and evaluate the constrained DCF's performance.

Composition of the Constrained DCF

If the zero-misfit DCF is uninvestable, then we must turn to an alternative form that will guide the construction of the invested DCF portfolio. That alternative is the constrained DCF. Computing the constrained DCF's composition involves a misfit-minimization problem.

The Constrained Misfit-Minimization Problem. If m non-DCF managers' policy allocations sum to w_{mgrs} (or $1 - w_{DCF}$), we can express this problem as one of building a benchmark, B_{m+1}, for manager $m + 1$ under a specified set of constraints that minimizes

$$\sigma^2_{misfit} = [T - (1 - w_{DCF})B^* - w_{DCF}B_{m+1}]' \qquad (6.3)$$
$$\sum [T - (1 - w_{DCF})B^* - w_{DCF}B_{m+1}],$$

where Σ is an $n \times n$ covariance matrix of all n securities contained in either the target or the managers' benchmarks.

We know from Equation 6.2 that $w_{DCF} B_{DCF} = T - (1 - w_{DCF}) B^*$, so on substitution into Equation 6.3, we want to find B_{m+1} that minimizes

$$\sigma^2_{misfit} = (w_{DCF}B_{DCF} - w_{DCF}B_{m+1})' \sum (w_{DCF}B_{DCF} - w_{DCF}B_{m+1}). \qquad (6.4)$$

Equation 6.4 can be rewritten as

$$\sigma^2_{misfit} = w^2_{DCF}\sigma^2_{track},$$

where

$$\sigma^2_{track} = (B_{DCF} - B_{m+1})' \sum (B_{DCF} - B_{m+1}). \qquad (6.5)$$

The term σ^2_{track} is the tracking error of B_{m+1} with respect to its ability to replicate the performance of the zero-misfit DCF (B_{DCF}).

Equation 6.5 emphasizes the importance of the zero-misfit DCF as it pertains to the constrained DCF. The DCF builder's task is to design a B_{m+1} benchmark, subject to any imposed constraints, that will best track the performance of the B_{DCF}. The performance benchmark will serve as the target for the DCF manager as he or she constructs the invested DCF portfolio.

Estimated Misfit for the Entire Investment Program. The final product of the misfit-minimization process is a benchmark for the entire investment program. The plan sponsor has assigned benchmarks and policy allocations for the non-DCF managers. The sponsor has also selected a DCF allocation. Having solved for the constrained DCF, we now have the last piece to the misfit-control puzzle. With the constrained DCF, we can create a total fund benchmark defined as

$$B_T = (1 - w_{DCF}) B^* + w_{DCF} B_{m+1}. \tag{6.6}$$

Prior to the start of an evaluation period, the DCF builder should be able to give the plan sponsor an estimate of the expected misfit risk for the investment program. That value is found by solving

$$E[\sigma^2_{misfit}] = (B_T - T)' \sum (B_T - T).$$

The plan sponsor's decision makers should understand the ramifications of the misfit risk present in its investment program. They should be aware of how its existing non-DCF manager structure and the limits on the constrained DCF affect the level of expected misfit risk. They must be willing to accept responsibility for the investment program's misfit.

Constraining the DCF. Constraints placed on the construction of B_{m+1} can be as varied as the circumstances dictate. Plan sponsors may insist that the constrained DCF own only long positions. Or, if short positions are permitted (usually for a specific group of securities), the constraints might include limits on the size of the portfolio's short component relative to the long component. Additional constraints could include limits on the weights assigned to specific securities or on the amount of portfolio turnover taking place from one rebalancing period to another. The plan sponsor, however, must recognize that as more constraints are placed on the DCF, its ability to reduce misfit risk is increasingly compromised.

The most common form of the constrained approximation to the zero-misfit DCF requires that all securities be held as non-negative positions (that is, no short selling). In that case, misfit minimization becomes a quadratic programming problem in which we want to find a vector of security weights,

$$w_{DCF} B_{m+1} = (x_1, x_2, x_3, \dots, x_n)' = \underline{X},$$

that minimizes

$$\sigma^2_{misfit} = [T - (1 - w_{DCF})B^* - \underline{X}]' \sum [T - (1 - w_{DCF})B^* - \underline{X}], \tag{6.7}$$

subject to $\underline{X}'1 = w_{DCF}$ (the budget constraint that the combined weight of the constrained DCF securities add to w_{DCF}) and $\underline{X} \geq 0$ (the constraint that forces the weights of the constrained DCF securities to be non-negative). Substituting from Equation 6.2, we can rewrite Equation 6.7 as

$$\sigma^2_{misfit} = (w_{DCF} B_{DCF} - \underline{X})' \sum (w_{DCF} B_{DCF} - \underline{X}). \tag{6.8}$$

In some situations, the plan sponsor or DCF manager may require that the DCF builder add further constraints on individual security positions. These constraints are expressed in the following form:

$$\underline{X}_{MIN} \le \underline{X} \le \underline{X}_{MAX},$$

wherein the lower limits (often set at zero) and upper limits (often related to liquidity) are placed on a specified list of securities eligible for inclusion in the constrained DCF.

A commercially available multifactor risk model provides the tool necessary to specify the covariance matrix found in Equations 6.7 and 6.8. That risk model, together with a quadratic programming algorithm (again, commercially available), a little algebra, and some variable transformations, are then used to compute the solution vector $\underline{X}$ and, hence, the constrained DCF.

The DCF's Cash Position

In Chapter 1, we briefly discussed the controversial subject of including cash in managers' benchmarks. At this point, our concern is how to handle manager benchmark cash (if it exists) in the construction of DCFs.

The simplest way to address cash in manager benchmarks and the target is to let it be the first element of those portfolios. In that case, cash is treated like any other security. Overweightings of cash in the aggregate manager benchmark relative to the target result in negative cash positions in the zero-misfit DCF. The converse holds if cash is underweighted in the aggregate manager benchmark relative to the target.

Alternatively, cash can be treated as a separate component of the aggregate manager benchmark and the DCF. We can express the cash and equity-only positions of the aggregate manager benchmark, the zero-misfit DCF, and the total fund benchmark, respectively, as

$$C_{B^*} + (1 - c_{B^*})B^*;$$
$$C_{DCF} + (1 - c_{DCF})B_{DCF};$$
$$C_T + (1 - c_T)T.$$

Recalling that the weights of the aggregate manager benchmark and the DCF in the total fund benchmark are $1 - w_{DCF}$ and w_{DCF}, respectively, we can simultaneously solve for the DCF's cash position, c_{DCF}, and the composition of the equity-only portion of the DCF, B_{DCF}. That solution gives

$$c_T = w_{DCF}c_{DCF} + (1 - w_{DCF})c_{B^*};$$
$$(1 - c_T)T = w_{DCF}(1 - c_{DCF})B_{DCF} + (1 - w_{DCF})(1 - c_{B^*})B^*.$$

If $w_{DCF} > 0$, then

$$c_{DCF} = \frac{c_T - (1 - w_{DCF})c_{B^*}}{w_{DCF}}$$

and

$$B_{DCF} = \frac{(1 - c_T)T - (1 - w_{DCF})(1 - c_{B^*})B^*}{w_{DCF}(1 - c_{DCF})}.$$

Under certain circumstances, it may be preferable to separate cash from the equity-only portion of the DCF. The DCF builder's job is to produce for the DCF manager an investable benchmark that has the lowest tracking error relative to the zero-misfit DCF, subject to any constraints. In several special cases, producing that investable, tight-tracking benchmark requires the DCF builder to manipulate the systematic risk exposure of the constrained DCF's equity-only component.

In the most common situation, the plan sponsor assigns a zero weight to cash in the target but the managers' benchmarks include positive cash allocations. As a result, cash has a positive misfit position, and therefore, $c_{DCF} < 0$. A negative cash position in the zero-misfit DCF implies a levered equity-only position. If the DCF manager is constrained to hold non-negative positions in all securities, including cash, then the DCF builder will have to intensify the systematic component of the equity-only constrained DCF to compensate for the levered zero-misfit DCF.

A similar situation occurs when the constrained DCF invests in futures contracts or engages in short selling. The DCF builder must include sufficient cash in the constrained DCF that the DCF can support initial margin positions and make any required margin calls without constantly selling and repurchasing portfolio securities. The calculation of those required cash positions is a complicated matter in itself, one that we will not address here. The increased cash position, however, causes a decline in the systematic risk of the total constrained DCF. The DCF builder must compensate for the change by increasing the systematic risk of the constrained DCF's equity-only portion.

Whether to work with the DCF's cash and equity-only portions separately or in a total portfolio context is a decision left to the DCF builder. In either case, cash is a special security (with zero volatility and low, but predictable, returns), which should be addressed and handled carefully in the DCF-construction process.

More on the Allocation to the DCF

So far, we have framed the DCF discussion as if the allocation to the DCF were

©The Research Foundation of the ICFA

determined outside of the misfit-control problem. Although that assumption was useful in allowing us to focus on other DCF issues, it is definitely unrealistic and undesirable. The choice of a DCF allocation has important implications for the rest of the investment program.

The VAM–Misfit Trade-Off. The allocation to the constrained DCF exhibits diminishing marginal benefits in misfit reduction. The first dollar invested provides the greatest impact, and subsequent dollars yield progressively smaller, but still positive, misfit reductions. If the invested DCF portfolio is passively managed, however, increasing the DCF's allocation linearly decreases the expected active-management return (or value-added return) for the investment program as more dollars are removed from the non-DCF managers.

Therefore, in determining its DCF allocation, the plan sponsor confronts a trade-off between misfit reduction and expected value added. Based on what we believe are realistic expected risk and reward parameters, Figure 6.1 illustrates that trade-off for a hypothetical investment program. Stated in annualized terms, in aggregate, the sponsor's four non-DCF managers have

Figure 6.1. The Effects of Altering the DCF's Allocation

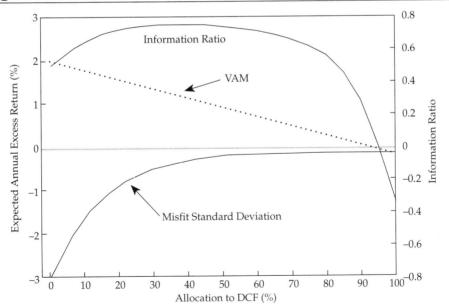

an expected value-added return of 2 percent with a volatility of 2.5 percent. The misfit risk associated with their aggregate manager benchmark is 3 percent. The DCF manager, in contrast, is expected to invest in a passively managed portfolio with a –0.10 percent expected value-added return and a 0.30 percent standard deviation.

The plan sponsor's misfit-control objective is to maximize the ratio of expected returns in excess of the target's returns relative to the volatility of those excess target returns. (Effectively, we are referring to an information ratio expressed in terms of returns relative to the target.) As shown in Figure 6.1, this "excess target" information ratio (measured on the right-hand axis) initially increases as the allocation to the DCF rises to about 25 percent. The excess target information ratio then flattens out over a wide allocation range and finally declines rapidly as the DCF allocation exceeds 75 percent. Figure 6.1 also indicates that the expected added value of the investment program falls in a linear progression as the DCF allocation grows. The investment program's misfit risk (measured on the left axis and expressed in [positive] standard deviation units) also declines but in a hyperbolic path toward zero as the DCF allocation increases.

The Two-Stage Approach to Determining the DCF's Allocation. How should the plan sponsor proceed in determining its desired DCF allocation? The most direct approach is to separate the problem into two stages: First, set the allocations to the non-DCF managers, and then choose the allocation to the DCF.

In the first stage, the plan sponsor selects its managers and assigns them policy allocations without any reference to the misfit problem. Recall that we recommended that the non-DCF manager allocations be determined through an analytical process called manager structuring. This process requires the sponsor to explicitly formulate assumptions about the managers' value-added capabilities, misfits, and the covariances among those variables. Those assumptions are used to derive an efficient set of allocations to the non-DCF managers.

The second stage of the DCF allocation problem takes the non-DCF managers' allocations determined in the first stage as fixed parameters. Assuming that the current allocations to those managers are somehow optimal, the sponsor will want to fund the DCF's allocation proportionately from each of the non-DCF managers. The aggregate of the managers' allocations displays known profiles of expected value added and misfit, which serve as inputs into the subsequent analysis. Essentially, the DCF builder uses the brute force technique of constructing a series of constrained DCFs across the feasible spectrum of DCF allocations at specified intervals. For example, constrained DCFs might be built based on DCF allocations ranging from 0 percent to 40 percent at 5 percent intervals, for a total of nine alternative allocation cases.

For each allocation case, estimates of the investment program's misfit risk, active-management risk, expected value-added returns, and a resulting excess target information ratio are computed. To enhance the analysis, the DCF builder can use a visual device similar to Figure 6.1. On receiving the results from these simulations, the plan sponsor must choose a DCF allocation that it believes offers an acceptable combination of expected value added and misfit. Our rule of thumb has been that sponsors should strive to reduce misfit risk below 1 percent a year. As can be seen in Figure 6.1, if that rule is followed, the plan sponsor usually will have considerable leeway in selecting its DCF allocation.

Applying any quantitative investment method literally, without the benefit of experience and intuitive insight, is usually unproductive. The process of selecting the DCF's allocation is no exception.[2] For example, in Figure 6.1, the optimal allocation occurs near 35 percent. Inspection of the graph indicates, however, that the difference in information ratios between a 25 percent allocation and a 35 percent allocation is immaterial and results in only an 11 bp difference in expected value added. Thus, a 25 percent allocation is probably satisfactory.

Our practical experience has been that DCF allocations in the range of 15–35 percent provide an appropriate level of misfit-risk reduction (usually by more than 50 percent if the DCF is constrained to hold only long positions) without excessively diminishing expected value added. If the constraints placed on the DCF are relaxed to allow as much as 30 percent short selling, misfit reductions in excess of 75 percent are often obtainable.

The Simultaneous Solution Approach to the DCF's Allocation. The two-stage approach to solving the DCF allocation problem is myopic, in that it ignores potentially valuable information about the value-added capabilities of the DCF manager and any relationships between the value-added and misfit processes of the DCF manager and the plan sponsor's individual non-DCF managers. Nevertheless, the two-stage approach has considerable appeal. The non-DCF managers are treated as a predetermined group whose joint purpose is to achieve the highest value-added information ratio. The DCF is

---

[2]In any optimization process, exploring the neighborhood around the optimal solution is important. Many solution spaces are rather flat near the optimal point. "Reasonable" solutions that are nearly optimal may have advantages over the optimal solution in ways that are not considered in the objective function.

viewed strictly as a risk-control tool. Both the non-DCF manager group and the DCF function in their assigned roles independently of one another. This two-step solution to the DCF allocation question is easier to calculate and explain to the plan's trustees than the more complex simultaneous solution.

The complete simultaneous solution involves jointly determining the individual non-DCF manager allocations, the DCF allocation, and the composition of the constrained DCF. This solution entails difficult mathematics, however, which is beyond the scope of this study. Because of the complexity of the analysis, plan sponsors are not likely to apply it.

In many ways, the choice between the two-stage solution and the simultaneous solution is similar to the portfolio-construction problems that balanced fund investment managers face.[3] Most balanced fund managers use their own two-stage approach. That is, they first set the allocation to stocks and bonds. Then, within each asset category, they select portfolios of securities. A more efficient but much more complex approach would be to simultaneously determine the composition of the stock and bond portfolios and, hence, the allocations to stocks and bonds. We are not aware of any institutional investment organizations managing balanced accounts that treat their stock and bond portfolios as one, however, for portfolio construction purposes.

---

[3]We alluded to this situation in Chapter 1 when we discussed the segregation of investment management responsibilities by asset category.

7. Extended DCF Topics

The completeness concept is a flexible framework that facilitates analysis of a wide range of investment management issues. By considering variations on the standard DCF theme, a plan sponsor can improve understanding of fundamental manager-structuring problems and develop an efficient multiple-manager investment program.

The Tactical Target

In the standard misfit-control problem, the plan sponsor uses a DCF to remain "style neutral"; that is, the sponsor wants its total portfolio to exhibit no significant investment style bias compared with the target. Consequently, the relative performance of particular styles should have no material impact on the investment program unless the plan sponsor's managers have collectively undertaken an active strategy of emphasizing one style or another.

Style Rotation. Some plan sponsors believe that they, or advisors hired by them, can forecast how certain investment styles will perform in the near term. On a long-term (or strategic) basis, they view the target as the appropriate focal point for their investment programs. On a short-term (or tactical) basis, however, they want to shift the exposures of their investment programs toward the favored style. "Style rotation" refers to this process of actively managing the style exposures of an investment program.[1] The DCF solution can easily be modified to accommodate this investment management technique and control unwanted misfit at the same time.

We will not debate the merits of style rotation here. Assume that the plan sponsor does indeed have skill in forecasting relative investment style performance. Also assume that the sponsor has retained a group of skillful active managers. None of these managers is a style rotator; each pursues its own distinct investment style.

The plan sponsor does not wish to disturb the investment activities of its current managers, whose aggregate manager benchmark is plotted in Figure 7.1 together with the target (which we will now call the strategic target). As

---

[1] For a discussion of investment issues involved in style rotation, see Jacobs and Levy (1996).

Figure 7.1. Style Rotation Using a DCF

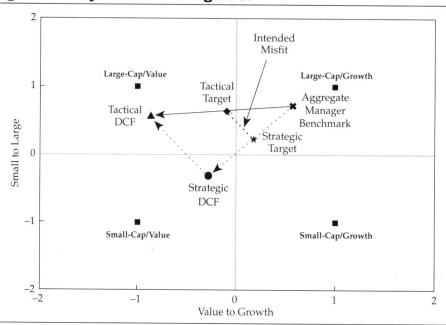

can be seen, the aggregate manager benchmark has a large-cap/growth bias relative to the strategic target. The problem is that the sponsor expects large-cap/value styles to outperform other investment styles during the next 12 months. The sponsor could take assets away from its managers with (large-cap or small-cap) growth styles and give those assets to other managers with large-cap/value styles. That approach might require considerable portfolio turnover, however, and would likely cause consternation among the manager team. Furthermore, when the sponsor next alters its style performance forecasts, the manager allocations would have to be adjusted again.

Strategic versus Tactical Targets. Essentially, the plan sponsor desires to establish a large-cap/value tactical asset category target (labeled "Tactical Target" in Figure 7.1). In the short-term, that portfolio represents the appropriate center of the investment program, not the strategic target. The sponsor now wishes to be style neutral relative to the tactical target, which will involve a large-cap/value bias relative to the strategic target. Just as the DCF can be used to create a style-neutral position relative to the strategic target, it can be applied similarly to a tactical target. The construction steps are exactly the same as those described in Chapter 3, but the tactical target is substituted for the strategic target.

Effectively, the plan sponsor has used the DCF to build misfit directly into its investment program. In this situation, however, the sponsor expects to be compensated for bearing misfit risk. In fact, the plan sponsor now has two sources of added value: the active-management skills of its managers and its own style-forecasting abilities.

In Equation 2.5, the plan sponsor sought a portfolio, $H = T - B^*$, such that

$$P^* = T + (B^* - T) + A^*$$

$$+ H = (T - B^*) + 0$$

$$\overline{}$$

$$P^* + H = T + 0 + A^*.$$

In the case of the tactical target, the plan sponsor wants to create a DCF that generates a specific misfit relative to the strategic target. If the tactical target is T_1, then the sponsor seeks a DCF portfolio, $H = T_1 - B^*$, such that

$$P^* = T + (B^* - T) + A^*$$

$$+ H = (T_1 - B^*) + 0$$

$$\overline{}$$

$$P^* + H = T + (T_1 - T) + A^*. \qquad (7.1)$$

Note that the desired misfit is $T_1 - T$, which is the difference between the tactical target and the strategic target. The T's in Equation 7.1 drop out, leaving the sponsor with the desired tactical style exposure and the value added by the managers; that is, $P^* + H = T_1 + A^*$.

Using the DCF to Implement Style Rotation. Without controlling misfit, a plan sponsor runs the risk that the style bias of the aggregate manager benchmark will adversely offset its style-rotation decisions. In our example, suppose the sponsor were to ignore the large-cap/growth bias of the active managers and simply invest additional assets in a large-cap/value indexed portfolio. If large-cap/growth stocks were to perform poorly as a group relative to the strategic target, the negative impact on the sponsor's total portfolio might overwhelm the positive effects of a correct style choice.

Some plan sponsors implement style rotation by hiring a manager to create a dedicated portfolio that tactically shifts style exposure based on the manager's forecasts of relative style performance. The DCF obviates the need for such a portfolio. The DCF functions as a swing manager, adjusting to a new tactical target without requiring revisions in the allocations to other managers. The sponsor may retain an advisor to direct the style-rotation process. All that advisor need do, however, is specify the tactical target. The

DCF manager then implements the style rotation by creating a portfolio that, when combined with the aggregate manager benchmark, yields the desired style exposure for the investment program.

The Fallacy of the Compensating Core

Chapter 2 described 10 approaches to dealing with the problem of misfit. One approach that was not discussed, but that has gained some notoriety, is known as the "compensating core." It offers an excellent example of how good intentions can yield to misguided implementation when practitioners ignore fundamental concepts.

Redefining Misfit (Incorrectly). On the surface, the compensating core is an enticing misfit-control approach. It involves essentially the same steps as the DCF approach with one major exception: Instead of creating an aggregate manager benchmark and calculating the misfit portfolio as $B^* - T$, it uses the aggregate of the managers' current portfolios and calculates misfit as $P^* - T$. After all, manager benchmarks can be troublesome for a plan sponsor to collect from the managers or, if need be, to produce directly. Why not avoid these practical difficulties and assume that the managers' actual portfolios adequately represent their investment styles?

Based on our simple portfolio algebra, we can immediately diagnose the logical error underlying the compensating core: Equation 1.3 describes the segmentation of a manager's portfolio into a style (benchmark) component and an active-management component; that is, $P = B + A$. Substituting the manager's portfolio, P, for the manager's benchmark, B, implies that $A = 0$; the manager makes no active-management decisions. This assumption is clearly unrealistic. Regardless of their investment skills, active managers are rarely accused of intentionally managing style index funds. Thus, assuming that their portfolios proxy for their benchmarks at any particular time makes little sense.

Part of the misinterpretation behind the compensating core comes from the observation that, over time, the manager's average portfolio will exhibit key financial characteristics similar to those of a well-designed benchmark. In fact, many benchmark builders rely on this feature. They observe a long series of the manager's past portfolios and construct the benchmark in such a way that it displays the same financial characteristics as the average values of the past portfolios. We have serious reservations about this approach and believe it should be tempered with information from other sources. Nevertheless, in many cases, this reliance solely on past portfolios does produce adequate manager benchmarks.

So, one can persuasively argue that a long series of past portfolios reflects the manager's investment style, but it is quite another thing to contend that a single portfolio accomplishes the same purpose. At any given time, P is likely to differ materially from B as the manager fulfills his or her active-management mandate. Those differences invalidate the compensating core solution.

Canceling Out the Managers' Active Decisions. What are the consequences of using a compensating core approach to misfit control as opposed to using a true DCF? Similar to Misfit Solution 9, the compensating core portfolio is calculated as that portfolio that directly offsets the misfit portfolio, except now misfit is defined as $P^* - T$ instead of $B^* - T$. Substituting this new definition into Equation 2.5, and remembering that $A^* = P^* - B^*$, gives

$$P^* = T + (B^* - T) + A^*$$

$$+ H = (T - P^*)$$

$$P^* + H = T + (B^* - T) + (P^* - B^*) + (T - P^*)$$

$$= T. \tag{7.2}$$

The combination of the aggregate manager portfolio and the compensating core portfolio now constitutes the plan sponsor's total portfolio. Equation 7.2 shows, however, that this combination equals the target itself; the sponsor has eliminated misfit but, at the same time, has created a target-based index fund by canceling all of the managers' active-management decisions. Unfortunately, this index fund pays active-management fees.

Figure 7.2 reinforces this message. It plots a hypothetical plan sponsor's aggregate manager benchmark and aggregate manager portfolio, together with the target. The aggregate manager portfolio and compensating core combination lie precisely on top of the target. Compare this outcome with that of the DCF approach. Figure 7.2 shows that the DCF portfolio is determined by the aggregate manager benchmark, not the aggregate manager portfolio. Moreover, the gap between the aggregate manager benchmark and aggregate manager portfolio represents the non-DCF managers' active-management decisions. The compensating core solution eliminates this gap, implying the cancellation of all active-management decisions.

Under the DCF solution, the plan sponsor's total portfolio is the combination of the DCF portfolio and the aggregate manager portfolio. Notice that the managers' active-management decisions remain in effect (except for a dilution caused by the allocation to the DCF). The sponsor gains control over misfit and continues to benefit from the expected value of the managers' investment skills.

Investment Style and Active Management. The lesson to be learned from the compensating core example is that successful misfit control requires

Figure 7.2. The Compensating Core

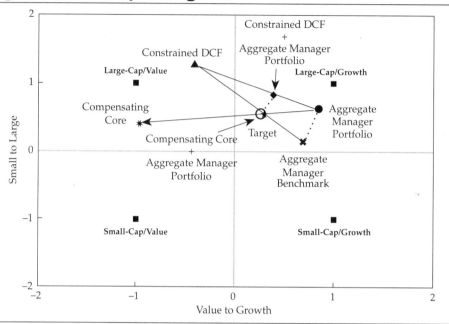

knowledge of the benchmarks of the plan sponsor's managers. Inadequate substitutes for those benchmarks will lead the misfit-control process astray. In the case of the compensating core, the managers' active decisions are eliminated, producing simply an expensive index fund.

Misunderstanding the difference between active management and investment style has led some plan sponsors to mistakenly believe that a DCF neutralizes active managers' investment judgments in the same way as the compensating core. Nothing could be farther from the truth. The DCF is designed strictly to eliminate the unintended style biases of the sponsors' active managers, as embodied in the aggregate of their benchmarks. It operates at the benchmark level, not at the active-portfolio level. Therefore, the composition of the DCF has no effect on the active-management decisions of a sponsor's managers. Indeed, the DCF permits a sponsor to be more aggressive (if it so chooses) in selecting the most skillful active managers without regard to their respective investment styles. The DCF compensates for any unwanted style biases created in the selection of active managers.

Manager Transitions

We certainly do not advocate that plan sponsors frequently reshuffle their alignment of non-DCF managers. Nevertheless, for a variety of reasons, adjustments to a plan sponsor's manager structure may become necessary. A DCF is a valuable tool to use in making those changes.

We often encounter situations in which a plan sponsor is reluctant to dismiss a poorly performing manager because of the impact the termination will have on the investment program's misfit. The sponsor is, correctly, concerned about unbalancing the style exposure of the aggregate manager benchmark, thereby increasing misfit risk. In this situation, the sponsor faces two difficult decisions: It must dismiss the existing manager and simultaneously identify a value-added manager who can provide the same style exposure. Ineffective managers are often able to retain their assignments for years simply because sponsors do not have the time or resources to locate a suitable replacement.

A DCF permits a plan sponsor to pay less attention to the misfit effects of changes in the non-DCF manager structure. Investment skill is a scarce resource. Selecting effective active managers is difficult enough for the sponsor without worrying as well about controlling misfit through the manager-selection process. With a DCF in place, a sponsor can make manager-hiring decisions based primarily on the managers' perceived investment skills.

The DCF can also assist the plan sponsor in limiting transition costs as it moves from one manager to another. For example, assume that the sponsor has decided to dismiss a large-cap/growth manager and hire a small-cap/value manager. The DCF can accommodate this transition by immediately taking on all of the outgoing manager's security holdings. As the aggregate manager benchmark shifts toward a smaller-cap and value orientation, the DCF will do just the opposite. The DCF will want to hold many of the large-cap/growth stocks acquired from the dismissed manager. Moreover, before the manager's dismissal, the DCF owned a certain proportion of small-cap/value stocks to offset the misfit of the large-cap/growth manager, now it will no longer include many of those stocks. They can be made available to the small-cap/value manager. Because the DCF holds securities on an informationless basis, the small-cap/value manager should find many stocks that he or she will want to include in his or her portfolio. These movements of securities between the DCF and the dismissed and hired managers involve no physical transactions; they exist only on the record books of the plan's custodian. The sponsor incurs no commissions and no market impact whenever it can use the intermediation facilities of the DCF.

Naturally, manager transitions are never as straightforward as this example implies. The new and the old managers will not hold securities in the same proportions as the DCF. Many open-market trades will still be required. Nevertheless, given the considerable expense associated with changing managers (estimates of 1–2 percent of the assets involved are typical), if the DCF can assist in reducing transition costs, it may reduce the drag that manager turnover can have on the investment program's performance.

The Augmented DCF

One of the disadvantages of investing in a DCF with a positive investment value (that is, either a plus-NAV/zero-misfit DCF or a constrained DCF) is the resulting dilution of the non-DCF managers' expected added value. In setting the DCF's allocation, the plan sponsor faces a trade-off: A larger DCF alloca-tion means less misfit risk but also a lower expected active-management return; a lower DCF allocation means more misfit risk but higher expected value-added return. Is it possible for the sponsor to have its cake and eat it too? The answer is yes, through a variation of the DCF concept called an "augmented DCF."

The plan sponsor's aggregate (non-DCF) manager portfolio can be expressed as $P^* = B^* + A^*$. We can think of the sponsor's total portfolio, N^*, as a combination of the aggregate manager portfolio and the zero-misfit DCF with the respective allocations $1 - w_{DCF}$ and w_{DCF}. This total portfolio is

$$N^* = (1 - w_{DCF})P^* + w_{DCF}B_{DCF}$$

$$= (1 - w_{DCF})(B^* + A^*) + w_{DCF}B_{DCF}$$

$$= (1 - w_{DCF})A^* + (1 - w_{DCF})B^* + w_{DCF}B_{DCF}. \qquad (7.3)$$

Equation 7.3 demonstrates that the total portfolio encompasses only a fraction, $1 - w_{DCF}$, of the managers' active-management decisions when the proportion w_{DCF} is allocated to the DCF. Recall that A^* is expressed as stock-by-stock under- and overweighted positions in the aggregate manager portfolio relative to the aggregate manager benchmark.

We would like to be able create a DCF portfolio that contains not only the security positions necessary to effect misfit control but also the active-management judgments of the non-DCF managers. That process is easier than it might first appear. Assume that the plan sponsor has made some arrangements with its non-DCF managers that permit it to copy their active-management strategies and transfer that information to other parts of the investment program.[2] Each month, the DCF builder is required to compare

---

[2] Previously, we assumed that the plan sponsor could not use the managers' value-added information to construct the DCF. That assumption has to be relaxed in order to construct the augmented DCF. Clearly, a special type of reporting arrangement would have to be established with the sponsor's managers to regularly access their value-added strategies.

the non-DCF managers' portfolios with their respective benchmarks and calculate the managers' aggregate value-added portfolio, A^*.

This active-management component, A^*, is a hedge portfolio. Because it has no net invested assets, we can always add A^* to any other portfolio—and without requiring the commitment of additional assets. So, the DCF builder adds A^* to the zero-misfit DCF, creating the augmented DCF; that is,

$$B_{AUG} = B_{DCF} + \delta A^*, \tag{7.4}$$

where δ is a scaling factor representing the "intensity" of the active-management decisions embedded in the augmented DCF. The augmented DCF is, therefore, nothing more than the zero-misfit DCF plus a fractional exposure to the non-DCF managers' active decisions.

From Equation 5.4, we know that the zero-misfit DCF (with normalized security weights that sum to 1) can be expressed as

$$B_{DCF} = \frac{[T - (1 - w_{DCF})B^*]}{w_{DCF}}. \tag{7.5}$$

Thus, we can rewrite Equation 7.4 as

$$w_{DCF}B_{AUG} = [T - (1 - w_{DCF})B_*] + w_{DCF}\,\delta A^*. \tag{7.6}$$

Combining the augmented DCF, as expressed in Equation 7.6, with the aggregate manager portfolio, P^*, from Equation 7.3 gives

$$(1 - w_{DCF})P^* = (1 - w_{DCF})B^* + (1 - w_{DCF})A^*$$

$$+ w_{DCF}B_{AUG} = [T - (1 - w_{DCF})B^*] + w_{DCF}\,\delta A^*$$

$$\rule{4cm}{0.4pt}$$

$$N^* = T + [1 - w_{DCF}(1 - \delta)]A^*. \tag{7.7}$$

When $\delta = 0$ (i.e., none of the non-DCF managers' active decisions are included in the augmented DCF), from Equation 7.7, the total portfolio becomes

$$N^* = T + (1 - w_{DCF})A^*,$$

which is our original diluted active-management result. When $\delta = 1$ (i.e., all the non-DCF managers' active decisions are included in the augmented DCF), even though the net investment in the DCF is positive, the total portfolio will be $N^* = T + A^*$, and there will be no dilution of active management across the total portfolio. We can even set $\delta > 1$, which will amplify the managers' active-management decisions in the total portfolio beyond what they would be in the absence of the DCF.

8. The Future of Misfit Control

The institutional investment community's understanding of misfit risk has come far in the past 20 years. Many organizations—plan sponsors, consultants, and money managers—have contributed to extending the body of knowledge in this obscure but important corner of the investment management world. We are confident that these advances will continue. Although we don't own a crystal ball, we are willing to make the following predictions:

- More plan sponsors will come to recognize and acknowledge the misfit problems present in their investment programs. With that increased recognition will come the need to monitor misfit. The advent of various types of style-analysis software has given sponsors desktop access to information on the investment styles of their managers. Sponsors will use that information to implement misfit-control procedures. Those procedures will vary significantly in terms of sophistication and effectiveness.

- Managers will take greater advantage of the opportunity to fill various niches missing from plan sponsors' investment programs. These managers will be capable of handling a broad range of custom assignments. They will accept benchmarks from their clients and apply their active-management skills to outperforming those benchmarks, within volatility ranges agreed to with the clients in advance.

- Long/short investing will continue to grow in acceptance. Managers who have disciplined value-added investment processes and who are capable of analyzing potentially thousands of securities for misvaluations will develop credible long/short investing track records. The advances in long/short investing will significantly enhance the effectiveness of misfit-control efforts.

- International equity will be the next frontier for misfit control. Effective international common stock risk models are becoming more widely available. Furthermore, as international equity becomes a greater portion of their investment programs, plan sponsors will be less willing to accept the inconsistencies between the investment styles of their managers and the universally assigned EAFE benchmark. The combination of these two trends will stimulate a demand for misfit analysis similar to that now applied at the domestic equity level.

- Creative applications of misfit-control techniques will be developed to address a wide range of portfolio-management issues. The use of tactical target DCFs in facilitating style rotation and augmented DCFs in enhancing active management are but two examples of these applications. Completeness concepts will be recognized as a critical component of an integrated approach to managing large pools of assets.

Appendix A: Deriving the Cost of Misfit Risk

How much cost does misfit risk inflict on a plan sponsor? Our simple algebraic portfolio segmentation assists in answering that question. Referring back to Equation 1.4, recall that a portfolio (be it a single manager's portfolio or an aggregation of portfolios) can be partitioned into three risk components: systematic, misfit, and active-management risk; that is, $P = T + (B - T) + A$.

Taking the variance of each side of that equation gives an expression for the total risk of the portfolio:

$$\text{Var}(P) = \text{Var}[T + (B - T) + A]. \tag{A.1}$$

From the benchmark orthogonality properties, we know that A is uncorrelated with either T or B. Therefore, Equation A.1 can be rewritten as

$$\text{Var}(P) = \text{Var}[T + (B - T)] + \text{Var}(A). \tag{A.2}$$

The first term on the right-hand side of Equation A.2 is the variance of the combined systematic and misfit components, which can be expressed as

$$\text{Var}[T + (B - T)] = \text{Var}(T) + \text{Var}(B - T) + 2\text{Cov}[T, (B - T)]$$
$$= \text{Var}(T) + \text{Var}(B - T) + 2[\text{Cov}(B, T) - \text{Var}(T)]. \tag{A.3}$$

The beta of any portfolio with respect to another portfolio represents the sensitivity of the return on the first portfolio to changes in the return on the second portfolio. Mathematically, we thus compute the beta of a benchmark portfolio, B, relative to the target portfolio, T, as

$$\beta_{B/T} = \frac{\text{Cov}(B, T)}{\text{Var}(T)}.$$

Therefore,

$$\text{Cov}(B, T) = \beta_{B/T} \times \text{Var}(T).$$

We can rewrite the variance of the combined systematic and misfit components from Equation A.3 to read

$$\text{Var}[T + (B - T)] = \text{Var}(T) + \text{Var}(B - T) + 2[\beta_{B/T} \times \text{Var}(T) - \text{Var}(T)]$$
$$= \text{Var}(T) + \text{Var}(B - T) + 2[\text{Var}(T) \times (\beta_{B/T} - 1)]. \tag{A.4}$$

110

One way to think about the extra risk that misfit introduces into a plan sponsor's portfolio is to "redeploy" it by creating a levered version of the target. The sponsor could own just the target and adjust the target's risk level to equal the risk associated with the combination of the target and misfit. The sponsor accomplishes that adjustment by borrowing funds to buy more of the target.[1]

Leverage results in an increase in both the beta and variance of a portfolio. With the beta of the levered target relative to the unlevered target referred to as $\beta_{L/T}$, the variance of the levered target becomes $(\beta_{L/T})^2 \text{Var}(T)$. So, replacing the left-hand side of Equation A.4 with the levered variance of the target gives

$$(\beta_{L/T})^2 \text{Var}(T) = \text{Var}(T) + \text{Var}(B-T) + 2[\text{Var}(T) \times (\beta_{B/T} - 1)]. \qquad (A.5)$$

Dividing both sides of Equation A.5 by $\text{Var}(T)$ gives

$$(\beta_{L/T})^2 = 1 + \frac{\text{Var}(B-T)}{\text{Var}(T)} + 2(\beta_{B/T} - 1). \qquad (A.6)$$

When $\beta_{B/T}$ Is Greater Than 1

The standard case is the situation in which $\beta_{B/T} \geq 1$. Although there is no economic requirement that this relationship must hold, as Figure 1.5 illustrates, the majority of domestic equity managers exhibit a greater growth orientation than do standard asset category targets. We found that the domestic equity investment programs of most plan sponsors exhibit a similar bias, which produces a $\beta_{B/T}$ greater than 1. (We examined 12 plan sponsors' domestic equity programs, and in 11 cases, this relationship held as expected.)

If $\beta_{B/T} \geq 1$, then restating Equation A.6, it must be true that

$$(\beta_{L/T})^2 \geq 1 + \frac{\text{Var}(B-T)}{\text{Var}(T)}$$

or

$$\beta_{L/T} \geq \left[1 + \frac{\text{Var}(B-T)}{\text{Var}(T)}\right]^{1/2}. \qquad (A.7)$$

We can now interpret the "cost" of misfit as the expected differential return associated with the beta of the levered portfolio. The investment program must earn this extra return to compensate for the increased risk that misfit produces. Because the beta of the target is assumed to be 1, the difference in betas between the levered target portfolio and the target is $\beta_{L/T} - 1$.[2] Applying the capital asset pricing model, whereby the expected return on a portfolio over the risk-free return is proportional to its beta times the expected return

---

[1]In standard investment textbook parlance, we are moving out along the capital market line.
[2]The target does not necessarily have to correspond to a broad-based, marketlike portfolio with a beta of 1. It might be quite different. In that case, we would have to introduce a market portfolio into the analysis, but the general conclusions would not be altered.

on the target over the risk-free return, gives the expected differential return generated by the levered portfolio.[3] Therefore,

Cost of misfit $= (\beta_{L/T} - 1)E(T - F)$.

Transforming Equation A.7 by subtracting 1 and multiplying by $E(T - F)$ yields a lower-bound expression for the cost of misfit; that is,

$$\text{Cost of misfit} \geq \left[1 + \frac{\text{Var}(B - T)}{\text{Var}(T)}\right]^{1/2} - 1 \times E(T - F). \tag{A.8}$$

When $\beta_{B/T}$ Is Less Than 1

Finding an investment program in which $\beta_{B/T} \leq 1$ would be unusual. Nevertheless, in that case, the plan sponsor is exposing itself to a lower level of systematic risk than that of the target. Because the target represents the plan sponsor's desired level of systematic risk, the shortfall causes the investment program to forgo the incremental return the market offers for accepting systematic risk; that is, the plan sponsor experiences a misfit cost associated with not accepting sufficient systematic risk. That cost is simply

$(1 - \beta_{B/T}) \times E(T - F)$.

We can show that the lower-bound expression for misfit cost (Equation A.8) also holds in this situation. The analysis is complicated by the fact that the right-hand side of Equation A.6 is not unambiguously positive, and thus, the expression for misfit cost may involve deleveraging as opposed to leveraging the target's return. Begin by dividing the benchmark B into its systematic, T, and unsystematic, X, components; that is,

$B = \beta_{B/T} T + X$.

By definition, the systematic portion of B is uncorrelated with the unsystematic portion, so $\text{Cov}(T,X) = 0$. Furthermore, by definition,

$\text{Cov}(B,T) = \beta_{B/T}\text{Var}(T)$.

Thus,

$\text{Var}(B) = (\beta_{B/T})^2\text{Var}(T) + \text{Var}(X)$.

---

[3]The capital asset pricing model states that the expected return on a portfolio equals $r_f + \beta_P[E(r_M) - r_f]$. In this application of the CAPM, the target serves as the market proxy.

Then, letting $k = \text{Var}(X)/\text{Var}(T)$,

$$\begin{aligned}
\text{Var}(B - T) &= \text{Var}[(\beta_{B/T} - 1)T + X] \\
&= (\beta_{B/T} - 1)^2 \text{Var}(T) + \text{Var}(X) \\
&= (\beta_{B/T} - 1)^2 \text{Var}(T) + k\text{Var}(T) \\
&= \text{Var}(T)[(1 - \beta_{B/T})^2 + k].
\end{aligned}$$

Hence,

$$\frac{\text{Var}(B - T)}{\text{Var}(T)} = (1 - \beta_{B/T})^2 + k$$

or

$$\left[1 + \frac{\text{Var}(B - T)}{\text{Var}(T)}\right]^{1/2} - 1 = [1 + (1 - \beta_{B/T})^2 + k]^{1/2} - 1 \leq [1 + (1 - \beta_{B/T})^2]^{1/2} - 1,$$

because $k \geq 0$.

Now, because $(1 + a^2)^{1/2} \leq (1 + a)$ for any $a \geq 0$, if $\beta_{B/T} < 1$ so that $a = (1 - \beta_{B/T})$, then

$$\begin{aligned}
\left[1 + \frac{\text{Var}(B - T)}{\text{Var}(T)}\right]^{1/2} - 1 &\leq 1 + (1 - \beta_{B/T})^2 - 1 \\
&\leq 1 - \beta_{B/T}
\end{aligned}$$

or

$$1 - \beta_{B/T} \geq \left[1 + \frac{\text{Var}(B - T)}{\text{Var}(T)}\right]^{1/2} - 1.$$

Therefore, similar to Equation A.8, the lower-bound expression for the cost of misfit in the case in which $\beta_{B/T} \leq 1$ is

$$\text{Cost of misfit} \geq \left[1 + \frac{\text{Var}(B - T)}{\text{Var}(T)}\right]^{1/2} - 1 \times E(T - F).$$

Appendix B: Financial Attributes of the Zero-Misfit DCF

Practitioners often describe portfolios in terms of such financial attributes as book-to-price ratios and dividend yields. For understanding the relationships among the financial attributes of the aggregate manager benchmark and those of the target and the zero-misfit DCF, the analogy of a see-saw is helpful. A heavy weight placed on one side of a see-saw can be balanced by a lighter weight on the other side only if that lighter weight is placed farther away from the fulcrum. In misfit control, the target serves as the fulcrum and the aggregate manager benchmark and the (normalized) zero-misfit DCF, B_{DCF}, are placed on opposite sides of the see-saw with weights of, respectively, $1 - w_{DCF}$ and w_{DCF}.

Assume for the moment that we are dealing with a plus-NAV version of the zero-misfit DCF so $w_{DCF} > 0$. If we examine any linear attribute of the target against the aggregate manager benchmark (such as the E/P, portfolio beta, or rate of return), the attribute difference weighted by $1 - w_{DCF}$ must be balanced by an attribute difference between the target and the DCF weighted by w_{DCF}. For example, let the return difference between the aggregate manager benchmark and the target be –2 percent and the weight of the non-DCF managers be 75 percent of the investment program. With only 25 percent allocated to the DCF, it must outperform the target by 6 percent in order to produce a zero-misfit return; that is,

(+6 percent $\times$ 0.25) + (–2 percent $\times$ 0.75) = 0.

This analysis also holds true when we consider portfolio betas. Using the same allocations, if the beta of the aggregate manager benchmark is 1.05 and the beta of the target is 0.99, then the beta of the zero-misfit DCF must be 0.81:

$[(0.81 - 0.99) \times 0.25] + [(1.05 - 0.99) \times 0.75] = 0$.

The limiting case of this analysis is reached with the zero-NAV/zero-misfit DCF. As w_{DCF} decreases, the DCF's financial attributes grow more pronounced. Fewer net assets are held in the DCF, whose weighted attributes must offset the misfit created by the aggregate manager benchmark. The increasingly extreme character of the DCF as its allocation declines is one reason why we caution against pushing that allocation too low.

When w_{DCF} reaches zero, the relationship expressed in Equation 5.2 and our see-saw analogy become inoperative. With a zero allocation, the DCF's average portfolio attributes are undefined. Like any hedge portfolio, however, the zero-NAV/zero-misfit DCF is still effectively exposed to various financial attributes. In such cases, we need to evaluate the long component of the DCF separately from the short component.[4] The weights of securities in each of these components can be expressed in non-negative terms, which allows the calculation of average attributes for the two components. Thus, we can define

$$H = H_{Long} - H_{Short}.$$

Applying Equation 5.2, the impact of the zero-NAV/zero-misfit DCF on the attributes of the investment program will arise as a weighted difference from

$$w_{DCF}B_{DCF} = w_{DCF,Long}B_{DCF,Long} - w_{DCF,Short}B_{DCF,Short},$$

where

$$w_{DCF} = w_{DCF,Long} - w_{DCF,Short}$$

$$B_{DCF,Long} = H_{DCF,Long}/w_{DCF,Long}$$

$$B_{DCF,Short} = H_{DCF,Short}/w_{DCF,Short}.$$

The Aggregate Manager Benchmark and the DCF

The see-saw analogy offers further insights if we consider the relationship between two difference-return series: the aggregate manager benchmark minus the target and the zero-misfit DCF minus the target. For the zero-misfit DCF to fulfill its assignment, the correlation of these difference-return series must be −1.0. Now, by definition,

$$\rho[(B^* - T),(B_{DCF} - T)] = \frac{\text{Cov}(B^* - T, B_{DCF} - T)}{\sqrt{\text{Var}(B^* - T) \times \text{Var}(B_{DCF} - T)}}. \tag{B.1}$$

From Equation 5.2, we can rearrange terms to get

$$B_{DCF} = \frac{[T - (1 - w_{DCF})B^*]}{w_{DCF}}. \tag{B.2}$$

---

[4]When the DCF builder constructs a constrained DCF that includes short selling, restating the construction problem in terms of separate long and short component portfolios, $B_{DCF,Long}$ and $B_{DCF,Short}$, is often more convenient than dealing directly with the combined portfolio.

Substituting Equation B.2 into the numerator of the right-hand side of Equation B.1 gives

$$\text{Cov}[(B^* - T),(B_{DCF} - T)] = \text{Cov}\left[B^* - T, \frac{T - (1 - w_{DCF})B^*}{w_{DCF}} - T\right]$$

$$= \text{Cov}\left[B^* - T, \frac{(1 - w_{DCF})}{w_{DCF}}(B^* - T)\right] \qquad (\text{B.3})$$

$$= -\left[\frac{1 - w_{DCF}}{w_{DCF}}\text{Var}(B^* - T)\right].$$

Similarly,

$$\text{Var}(B_{DCF} - T) = \left[\frac{1 - w_{DCF}}{w_{DCF}}\right]^2 \text{Var}(B^* - T). \qquad (\text{B.4})$$

Substituting Equations B.3 and B.4 into Equation B.1 and dividing by the term $\text{Var}(B^* - T)$ gives us this result:

$$\rho[(B^* - T),(B_{DCF} - T)] = -1.$$

If the zero-misfit DCF is properly positioned on the see-saw, its return versus the target must be perfectly negatively correlated with the misfit portfolio. The DCF's negative correlation with the misfit portfolio causes it to underperform the target when the non-DCF managers' investment styles, in aggregate, are performing well relative to the target, and vice versa. Thus, quite appropriately, one practitioner has dubbed the DCF "the ultimate contrarian."

Relative Return Variability of the Zero-Misfit DCF

Equation B.4 conveys another important point. Given both the DCF's allocation, w_{DCF}, and the variability of misfit return (which can easily be estimated), we know the variability of the zero-misfit DCF's return relative to the target. As we increase the DCF's allocation, the variability of the zero-misfit DCF's relative return declines. Taking the square root of both sides of Equation B.4 shows that if $w_{DCF} = 0.1$, then the standard deviation of the zero-misfit DCF's relative return is 9 times that of the misfit return. Increasing the DCF's allocation to 0.2 reduces the multiple to 4, and an allocation of 0.4 yields a multiple of 1.5.

Some plan sponsors' decision makers are uncomfortable with high levels of DCF return variability. They may be concerned that the plan's trustees do not fully understand the risk-control function that the DCF serves. In light of the DCF's negative correlation with the misfit portfolio, these trustees may misinterpret (and react adversely to) a situation in which the DCF significantly underperforms the target even though that underperformance may be precisely what a DCF portfolio with a small allocation must produce to offset a positive misfit return. This issue of DCF return variability is another reason we advise against excessively small DCF allocations.

Glossary

Active management: A form of investment management that involves buying and selling securities with the objective of outperforming a specified benchmark.

Active-management return: The return on a manager's portfolio earned in excess of the manager's benchmark return (also referred to as the value of active management or value-added return).

Active-management risk: The variability of a manager's active-management return. Usually expressed as an annualized standard deviation.

Aggregate manager benchmark: The weighted combination of the benchmarks of all non-DCF managers involved in a plan sponsor's investment program. The benchmarks' weights represent the managers' respective policy allocations.

Asset category: A broad collection of securities possessing similar fundamental attributes that distinguish them from other groups of securities.

Asset category target (target): A set of securities and their associated weights from a particular asset category that the plan sponsor believes best achieves the purposes for which the asset category is being included in the plan's investment policy.

Benchmark: A set of securities and associated security weights that provides a passive representation of a manager's investment process.

Constrained DCF: A portfolio of securities, designed to replicate the performance of the zero-misfit DCF, whose composition is restricted by a set of specified criteria. It serves as the benchmark for the DCF manager.

DCF slippage: The slight difference between expected misfit return or risk and realized misfit return or risk caused by factors exogenous to the misfit-control process.

Dynamic completeness fund (DCF): A portfolio custom designed to control the misfit present in a plan sponsor's investment program.

Excess target return: The return on a portfolio earned in excess of the target's return.

Excess target risk: The variability of a portfolio's excess target return—usually expressed as an annualized standard deviation.

Hedge portfolio: A portfolio with no net asset value. The positive value of long positions in the portfolio are exactly offset by the negative value of short positions.

Information ratio (IR): The ratio of active-management return to active-management risk.

Invested DCF: A portfolio constructed and maintained by the DCF manager that is designed to at least match the returns on the constrained DCF.

Investment policy: Procedures that guide the management of a plan sponsor's assets, as well as express the philosophy and goals of the plan sponsor with regard to managing the plan's assets.

Investment skill: The ability to construct portfolios with returns that exceed those of an appropriate benchmark on a statistically significant basis.

Investment style: A general description of the types of securities that a manager typically holds.

Manager structuring: The process of systematically assigning policy weights to the investment managers within an investment program based on the expected active and misfit returns and risks associated with the managers.

Misfit: The difference between an aggregate manager benchmark (or an individual manager's benchmark) and the target (also referred to as style bias).

Misfit portfolio: The stock-by-stock difference in security weights between the aggregate manager benchmark and the target.

Misfit return: The difference in returns between an aggregate manager benchmark (or an individual manager's benchmark) and the return on the target.

Misfit risk: The variability of an aggregate manager benchmark's (or an individual manager benchmark's) misfit return—usually expressed as an annualized standard deviation (also referred to as style risk).

Passive management: A form of investment management that involves buying and holding securities with the objective of matching the performance of a specified benchmark.

Plus-NAV/zero-misfit DCF: The version of the zero-misfit DCF in which the value of the long positions exceeds that of the short positions so that the DCF has a positive invested value.

Style bias: The difference between an aggregate manager benchmark (or an individual manager's benchmark) and the target (also referred to as misfit).

Style risk: The variability of an aggregate manager benchmark's (or an individual manager benchmark's) misfit return—usually expressed as an annualized standard deviation (also referred to as misfit risk).

Value of active management (VAM): The return on a portfolio earned in excess of the benchmark's return (also referred to as active-management return or value-added return).

Value-added return: The return on a portfolio earned in excess of the benchmark's return (also referred to as active-management return or the value of active management).

Zero-misfit DCF: The DCF portfolio that, on a stock-by-stock basis, eliminates all misfit (*ex ante*) in an investment program.

Zero-NAV/zero-misfit DCF: The version of the zero-misfit DCF in which the value of the long positions precisely offsets the value of the short positions so that the DCF has no invested value.

References

Ambachtsheer, Keith D. 1977. "Where Are the Customers' Alphas?" *Journal of Portfolio Management*, vol. 4, no. 1 (Fall):52–56.

———. 1986. *Pension Funds and the Bottom Line: Managing the Corporate Pension Fund as a Financial Business*. Homewood, IL: Dow Jones Irwin.

Bailey, Jeffery V. 1992. "Evaluating Benchmark Quality." *Financial Analysts Journal*, vol. 48, no. 3 (May/June):33–39.

Bailey, Jeffery V., Thomas M. Richards, and David E. Tierney. 1988. "Benchmark Portfolios and the Manager/Plan Sponsor Relationship." *Journal of Corporate Finance*, vol. 4, no. 4 (Winter):25–32.

———. 1990. "Concept and Design." In *Managing Institutional Assets*. Edited by Frank J. Fabozzi. New York: Harper & Row.

BARRA. 1989. "Comparison of the Capitalization- and Equal-Weighted S&P 500." *BARRA U.S. Newsletter* (February):9–12.

Barry, Christopher B., and Laura T. Starks. 1984. "Investment Management and Risk Sharing with Multiple Managers." *Journal of Finance*, vol. 39, no. 2 (June):477–91.

Chopra, Vijay K., and William T. Ziemba. 1993. "The Effect of Errors in Means, Variances, and Covariances on Optimal Portfolio Choice." *Journal of Portfolio Management*, vol. 19, no. 2 (Winter):6–11.

Divecha, Arjun, and Richard C. Grinold. 1989. "Normal Portfolios: Issues for Sponsors, Managers, and Consultants." *Financial Analysts Journal*, vol. 45, no. 2 (March/April):7–13.

Ellis, Charles D. 1985. *Investment Policy*. Homewood, IL: Dow Jones Irwin.

Fama, Eugene F., and Kenneth R. French. 1992. "The Cross-Section of Expected Stock Returns." *Journal of Finance*, vol. 47, no. 2 (June):427–66.

Greer, Robert J. 1997. "What Is an Asset Class, Anyway?" *Journal of Portfolio Management,* vol. 23, no. 2 (Winter):86–91.

Grinold, Richard C. 1989. "The Fundamental Law of Active Management." *Journal of Portfolio Management*, vol. 15, no. 3 (Spring):30–37.

———. 1992. "Are Benchmark Portfolios Efficient?" *Journal of Portfolio Management*, vol. 19, no. 1 (Fall):34–40.

Haugen, Robert A., and Nardin L. Baker. 1991. "The Efficient Market Inefficiency of Capitalization-Weighted Stock Portfolios." *Journal of Portfolio Management*, vol. 17, no. 3 (Spring):35–40.

Jacobs, Bruce I., and Kenneth N. Levy. 1993. "Long/Short Equity Investing." *Journal of Portfolio Management*, vol. 20, no. 1 (Fall):52–63.

———. 1996. "High-Definition Style Rotation." *Journal of Investing*, vol. 5, no. 3 (Fall):14–23.

Jeffrey, Robert H. 1991. "Do Clients Need So Many Portfolio Managers?" *Journal of Portfolio Management*, vol. 18, no. 1 (Fall):13–19.

Kritzman, Mark. 1986. "How to Detect Skill in Management Performance." *Journal of Portfolio Management*, vol. 13, no. 2 (Winter):16–20.

Michaud, Richard O. 1989. "The Markowitz Optimization Enigma: Is 'Optimized' Optimal?" *Financial Analysts Journal*, vol. 45, no. 1 (January/February):31–42.

Sharpe, William F. 1981. "Decentralized Investment Management." *Journal of Finance*, vol. 36, no. 2 (May):217–34.

———. 1992. "Asset Allocation: Management Style and Performance Measurement." *Journal of Portfolio Management*, vol. 18, no. 2 (Winter):7–19.

———. 1994. "The Sharpe Ratio." *Journal of Portfolio Management*, vol. 21, no. 1 (Fall):49–58.

Tierney, David E., and Kenneth J. Winston. 1990. "Defining and Using Dynamic Completeness Funds to Enhance Total Fund Efficiency." *Financial Analysts Journal*, vol. 46, no. 4 (July/August):49–54.

———. 1991. "Using Generic Benchmarks to Present Manager Styles." *Journal of Portfolio Management*, vol. 17, no. 4 (Summer):33–36.

Winston, Kenneth J. 1993. "The 'Efficient Index' and Predictions of Portfolio Variance." *Journal of Portfolio Management*, vol. 19, no. 3 (Spring):27–34.

Selected AIMR Publications

AIMR Performance Presentation Standards Handbook, 2nd edition, 1996

Deregulation of the Electric Utility Industry, 1997

Economic Analysis for Investment Professionals, 1997

Finding Reality in Reported Earnings, 1997
Jan R. Squires, CFA, *Editor*

Global Bond Management, 1997
Jan R. Squires, CFA, *Editor*

Global Equity Investing, 1996

Global Portfolio Management, 1996
Jan R. Squires, CFA, *Editor*

Implementing Global Equity Strategy: Spotlight on Asia, 1997

Investing in Small-Cap and Microcap Securities, 1997

Investing Worldwide VIII: Developments in Global Portfolio Management, 1997

Managing Currency Risk, 1997

Merck & Company: A Comprehensive Equity Valuation Analysis, 1996
Randall S. Billingsley, CFA

Readings in Venture Capital, 1997

Standards of Practice Casebook, 1996

Standards of Practice Handbook, 7th edition, 1996

A full catalog of publications is available on AIMR's World Wide Web site at **www.aimr.org**; or you may write to AIMR, P.O. Box 3668, Charlottesville, VA 22903 U.S.A.; call 1-804-980-3668; fax 1-804-963-6826; or e-mail **info@aimr.org** to receive a free copy. All prices are subject to change.